P9-AFI-094

Yale Studies in English

Benjamin Christie Nangle, Editor

Volume 147

*Published with aid from the foundation
established in memory of Philip Hamilton McMillan
of the class of 1894, Yale College*

THE PASTORAL ART

OF ROBERT FROST

by John F. Lynen

New Haven: YALE UNIVERSITY PRESS, 1960

© *1960 by Yale University Press, Inc.*
Set in Baskerville type and
printed in the United States of America by
Vail-Ballou Press, Inc., Binghamton, N.Y.
All rights reserved. This book may not be
reproduced, in whole or in part, in any form
(except by reviewers for the public press),
without written permission from the publishers.
Library of Congress catalog card number: 60-7826

Frost quotations are reprinted by permission of
Henry Holt and Company, Inc. from *Complete
Poems of Robert Frost,* copyright 1930, 1939, 1943,
1947, 1949 by Henry Holt and Company, Inc., copyright 1936, 1942, 1945 by Robert Frost.

"When My Five and Country Senses See" is reprinted on pp. 182–3 by permission of New Directions from *The Collected Poems of Dylan Thomas,*
copyright 1939, 1942, 1946 by New Directions.

TO CLEANTH BROOKS

PREFACE

THE EXPERIENCE of reading poetry must always be subjective, and anyone who undertakes to describe a poet's work will therefore be suspected of attempting to substitute his own views for the reader's. The poets whose work we know give us the added satisfaction of a proprietary interest. Probably most persons who open this book will have already in their imaginations an unwritten volume entitled *My Robert Frost,* and the present work will have to meet the test of comparison with that more authoritative text. This is as it should be, for poetry engages the whole personality; to read it at all we must read it subjectively. Yet granting this, and it is a great deal, we must also admit that poetry is something in itself, not just our view of it or any combination of personal views. The historian who seeks to discover the allegorical allusions in Virgil's tenth eclogue assumes that there is a poem to be interpreted, however much he may appeal to the historical vicissitudes the poem has suffered; and the ordinary reader, when he declares that he does not understand a poem by Yeats or Stevens, tacitly makes the same concession. Few will maintain, except as a curious paradox in philosophy, that a poem lost for centuries and then rediscovered ceased to exist as a poem in the fullest sense during the interval when it was unknown. The objective being of poetry is as necessary to the reader's experience as his subjective response. The solution of this contradiction attends the solution of everything. Meanwhile, it is more useful to discuss poems than responses.

The present work is an attempt to describe some of the
more important facts of Frost's art. It would be less than
human not to hope that the reader will find himself in
agreement, but I have been acutely aware that he, looking
at things from a different angle of vision, may see the objective truth in a quite different light. For this reason, I
have been less concerned to win him to see Frost as I do
than to suggest a new way of approaching his poetry.

Certainly the old way is familiar enough. It has, in fact,
encouraged a uniformity of opinion which does no honor
to the radical individualism many of Frost's critics pro-
claim and the poet himself so honestly exemplifies. Here,
if anywhere, "monolithic solidarity" should be suspect.
Far from challenging the reader's version of *My Robert
Frost,* I only ask him to consider whether it is really his
own or the one so frequently reproduced in the reviews.

The view of Frost presented in the following pages is
designed to allow for the widest possible range of reader
experience. A great many poems are discussed in detail,
but always with the intent of illustrating *how* Frost writes
rather than of offering a final interpretation of *what* he
says. Essentially, then, this is a study of his poetic form.
Since formal criticism has of late been much attacked
(often, one notes, by those who are glad enough to use the
methods they condemn), I had better say a word or two
in explanation of why I have chosen to approach the poet
in this way. Form, as I conceive it, is inseparable from the
content or thought of a poem, nor would I deny for a
moment that our most important concern is the meaning
a poem expresses rather than its texture or technical details. But it seems to me that the meaning of a Frost poem
—or any good poem—is quite a complicated thing and
cannot be found in any one overt statement the poet may
make, either in the poem or outside it. The only way we
may do that meaning justice is to seek it in the poem as a

whole, in the relationships between all of its statements, in other words, in the form. The alternative approach—and it is the one favored by most of Frost's critics—is to formulate what is called the poet's "thought," and then apply it to the individual poems. But how are we to discover what Frost's "thought" is? The usual method is to collect his stated opinions as they are found in his writings, lectures, and conversation. The result is a set of lucid abstractions: Frost's ideas about love, about patriotism, about education, etc. Certainly these cast some light on the poems, yet I suspect that they also confuse our vision of them, as by too bright a reflection. Too often, what happens is that the critic merely "gets back" from the poem the idea he had assumed beforehand was there, and only that idea. Yet there is an even greater danger than this, the danger of ignoring all but the poet's stated ideas. To me it seems axiomatic that poetry expresses thoughts which lie far above and far below the level of conscious opinion. That is why a freethinker can admire Dante and a radical Tennyson. Many of our best poets have had commonplace opinions or scarcely any worth mentioning.

This, of course, is not true of Frost, who is for our time the poet of ideas *par excellence,* one who likes to express ideas openly in his verse, and sometimes pours them forth in such a deluge one suspects him of puckishly inverting MacLeish's definition to read, "A poem should not be, but mean." His ideas are consistently interesting, even for those who cannot accept them, and thus in reading him it is more important than ever to remember that stated ideas in poetry are as colors in painting, the material rather than the meaning. If we insist on taking them for the meaning, we will have some original and brilliant notions, but not the poetry, which is infinitely more valuable.

I dwell upon these elementary points at the risk of offending the many readers for whom they are tiresomely

familiar, because even the best-informed seem to have
trouble looking beyond Frost's "thought" to the rich complexity of his poetic meaning. The error is not so much the
obvious one of reading out of context as that of reading
only on the level of ideas, the level, for example, which the
following lines occupy:

> Only where love and need are one,
> And the work is play for mortal stakes,
> Is the deed ever really done
> For Heaven and the future's sakes.

In itself, this is an interesting, even important idea, enjoy-
able to think about as we go back to the office on a Monday
morning. It will help too in our reading of a few other
Frost poems on work, "Mowing" and "The Star-Splitter,"
for instance. Yet it does not represent the meaning of "Two
Tramps in Mud Time," even though it comes in at the
end of that poem as a sort of moral. We must see it in relation to the earlier parts, the wonderful description at the
beginning of chopping wood in the warm sunshine, the
pleasant yet uncertain April weather, the two loitering
tramps from "God knows where" and their needy claim
upon the work the poet does half for pleasure. The poem's
meaning is the picture of reality it gives us, and the final
idea is but the boldest stroke in this composition. It doesn't
really matter whether we agree that love and need should
be one; what counts is the vision this helps to create. And
if we insist upon equating the meaning with an idea, let us
take rather the more fundamental and more profound one
which underlies the whole poem: Frost's concept of the
mind's power to unify all the aspects of experience. This
is a far more important matter in Frost than the final
statement of this poem. It is implicit in most of his poems,
lies at the center of his regionalism and enters into the very
form of his verse, yet in a catalogue of stated opinions it
would, at best, be only one more item on the list. If Frost's

thought is our primary concern, let us take care in defining it. To do so, we must attend very closely to his mode of statement, and thus, in the end, to his poetic form.

The indebtedness of this book to William Empson will be apparent to anyone who has come to know his brilliant study, *English Pastoral Poetry*. The general view of pastoral here presented is directly based upon his, which, in turn, seems to be derived from a few very cogent paragraphs in Sir Walter Greg's *Pastoral Poetry and Pastoral Drama*. Needless to say, without Empson's work mine would not have been possible, but at the same time it seems appropriate here to point out certain modifications of his view which seemed to me necessary. Empson's approach is essentially sociological: he describes pastoralism as a literary form growing up under certain social conditions and serving to reconcile, on the level of attitudes, at least, the conflicts which result from class divisions. My own concern is less with the social matrix of pastoralism, and in considering the pastoral art of various periods I have become persuaded that class relationships are not so important to the genre as the need individuals have felt to measure their complex society by the standards of a simple one. Furthermore Empson extends the definition of pastoral to include kinds of literature remote from the poetry of rural life—*The Beggar's Opera* and *Alice in Wonderland,* for example. Admittedly, definitions are a matter of convenience, but too broad a definition can be as inconvenient as too narrow. Rural life, it would seem, is the essential subject matter of pastoral, for only here do we find that blending of the social and the natural orders to form the little world by which the pastoralist evaluates experience. Without the swain there can be no pastoral, yet both he and his world can be pictured as effectively in Devonshire or New England as in the lands of the classical eclogue. So that while insisting upon the rural nature of pastoralism, we should allow it the diversity with regard

to scenery and character which from Virgil onward it en-
joyed in the old tradition. If Empson has pushed the idea
of pastoral even beyond this ample limit, this too has been
a service in that it helps us to distinguish the essential elements of the form from its merely conventional trappings.

To Cleanth Brooks I owe an even larger debt of gratitude. In its original form this work was a dissertation
submitted to the Yale Graduate School in partial fulfillment of the requirements for the Ph.D. At the outset, his
suggestions crystallized the rather confused ideas about
Frost's poetry I was attempting to put in order, and in the
several years since, he has given me generously of his time
and counsel. His insights have made easy problems I could
not otherwise have resolved, and on those occasions when
our opinions differed, I have had his always reasonable
and persuasive views against which to measure the diverg-
ence of my own.

Among the many others who have helped me, I am
obliged in particular to Norman Holmes Pearson for supplying certain materials on Frost and to Donald E. McCoy
for contributing several items to the bibliography. I am
also grateful to the Fund for Young Scholars for providing
substantial funds toward publication. Finally, I wish to
express my thanks to Henry Holt & Co. for their generosity
in allowing me to quote freely from the poet's work.

In the bibliography, I have attempted to provide a useful reference list rather than a complete survey. Only the
most important editions of Frost and what seemed to me
the more significant or historically representative writings
about him are included. Under miscellaneous poetry and
prose, only those works by Frost not available in collected
editions are given. The list of explications is for convenient
reference; many others are to be found in works mentioned
elsewhere in the bibliography.

March, 1960   J.F.L.

CONTENTS

CHAPTER 1

THE PASTORAL MODE:
SYMBOLISM AND PERSPECTIVE

Robert Frost occupies a unique position in modern poetry. Unlike most contemporary poets, he has managed to win a wide popular audience while earning the almost universal acclaim of critics and scholars. There are doubtless three or four other modern poets whose claims to a permanent place in our literature are equally secure, but none is better known than Frost, and few, if any, better loved. Yet despite this wide recognition he has not received the careful critical evaluation his work deserves. The reader who takes the trouble to leaf through the numerous articles and the half dozen or so books which have so far appeared will find much in the way of biographical sketch, regional vignette, and appreciation, but very few efforts to explore the poetry itself. Apparently Frost's own personality and the New England he depicts in many of his best poems are so interesting in themselves that critics have tended to focus attention upon these subjects, with the result that what are really the most important things—the poems he has written and the special qualities of his writing—have been little studied.

The main cause of this neglect, however, is to be found in the very nature of Frost's art. The poetry he has written is of a kind distinctly different from that of his major con-

temporaries. On the surface, his work has a disarming simplicity which sets it apart. We are accustomed to certain
obscurities of style in modern poetry—fragmentary sentences, irregular verse forms, abrupt shifts from subject to
subject, and an elliptical mode of reference. Frost's sentences are always clear, his verse forms traditional, his language close to everyday speech—no obscurity here, no
oblique glances at Dante and the Book of Revelation, no
esoteric learning or thickets of private symbolism. Because
he demands less erudition in the reader, his poetry may
seem to lack the complexity of thought one finds at the
center of the best modern verse. We expect in modern
poetry an ironic view and find Frost whimsical or jocular;
we expect an awareness of paradox and find him offering
confident opinions; we expect a tension of feelings and find
him writing in the relaxed mood of conversation; we expect bold metaphor and find him indulging in playful com-
parisons; we expect myth and find that he gives us anecdote. The illusion of simplicity is so strong that it is hard
to place Frost in the present century, and one is therefore
tempted to assume that he is a belated Victorian writing in
a manner so familiar and well-understood that there is no
need to examine his methods as a poet.

The simplicity, however, is only apparent. If "An Old
Man's Winter Night" does not seem to call for the kind of
careful exegesis required by Eliot's "Sweeney Among the
Nightingales," this does not mean that it is a simple poem;
it means only that Frost's poem appears to be less complex
than it really is. Eliot deals with major themes in a pro-
fessedly serious way, so that the reader is made alert to the
difficulties of interpretation. Frost, on the other hand,
seems merely to describe impressions isolated in the moment of perception. The result is that his poems may be
read as pure description; and if they seem unusually good,
this may be attributed to nothing more than accurate re-

porting. The real difficulty of Frost only becomes apparent when the reader pauses at the end of such a poem as "An Old Man's Winter Night," "Mending Wall," or "Stopping by Woods on a Snowy Evening" and asks, "What does the poem mean?"

Take, for example, the last. On the surface it is no more than a simple anecdote relating how the poet pauses one evening along a country road to watch the snow fall in the woods: "The woods are lovely, dark and deep," and as he sits in his sleigh gazing into the soft, silent whiteness he is tempted to stay on and on, allowing his mind to lose itself in the enchanted grove.[1] His consciousness seems on the verge of freeing itself from ordinary life, as if it were about to dissolve in the shadowy blank, but his mind holds back from this. He remembers that his journey has a purpose. He has promises to keep and many miles to go before he can yield to the dreamlike release which the woods seem to offer.

This is the core of the poem, a moving personal experience exquisitely rendered. Yet in reconsidering it one cannot quite shake off the feeling that a good deal more is intended. The poem is not just a record of something that once happened to the poet; it points outward from the moment described toward far broader areas of experience. It expresses the conflict, which everyone has felt, between the demands of practical life, with its obligations to others, and the poignant desire to escape into a land of reverie, where consciousness is dimmed and the senses are made independent of necessity. There is no overt symbolism in "Stopping by Woods," and yet the reader finds his vision directed in such a way that he sees the poet's purely per-

1. All quotations from Frost's poetry are taken from *Complete Poems of Robert Frost: 1949*, New York, Henry Holt, 1949. This is the most recent and most authoritative complete edition. Since it also has the advantage of an index, page and line references are provided only in a few special cases.

sonal experience as an image of experiences common to all. The wide scope of the meaning becomes obvious in the final lines. These state the conflict in a simple, realistic way: the poet will have to fulfill certain duties, perhaps just chores about the farm, before he can go to bed; but the "promises," the "sleep," and the "miles to go" widen to include more important aspects of his life and, further, elements of every man's life. Sleep here is, of course, the well-earned reward at the end of a day's work; but reaching out beyond this, as indeed the whole poem transcends its rural setting, the idea of sleep merges with the final sleep, death itself. It stands in contrast to the snowy woods, whose temptation is to an irresponsible indulgence ending in the loss of consciousness: it is normal death, the release at the end of a life in which man has kept his promises and traveled the whole journey through human experience.

The interpretation here offered will not seem new or surprising. The poem is a familiar one, and most readers will have read it and read about it many times.[2] For our present purposes this is an advantage, for since the general meaning of the poem is clear we can turn our attention to the problem of just how this meaning is conveyed. As I have said, there are no pointed symbols, no literary parallels or signposts to guide us, much less a clear statement on the poet's part indicating the direction of his thought. The wider areas of meaning seem completely taken up within the particular incident. This does not mean that the poem is the simple description it appears. One cannot dismiss the persistent feeling that more is involved, and indeed if the poem is read only as a series of flat, factual statements, it makes no sense at all. The fact that "The woods are lovely, dark and deep" has no clear logical connection with Frost's next assertion, "But I have promises

2. See, for example, John Ciardi, "Robert Frost: The Way to The Poem," *Saturday Review of Literature* (April 12, 1958), pp. 13-15, 65.

to keep," unless one moves from the descriptive level to a more distant range of meaning and recognizes that looking at the woods signifies more than idling too long by the roadside, the promises more than a few domestic duties. Otherwise the problem the poet faces would be too trivial to command much interest—he could while away ten minutes watching the snow fall and still get home in time to milk the cows. Similarly, the way the horse seems to wonder why the man has stopped is a trifling irrelevance if taken only as a descriptive detail; but it has the important function in the poem of establishing a contrast—one that continually interests Frost—between the merely natural and the human. The animal's inability to conceive anything beyond the practical concerns of food and shelter emphasizes man's love of reverie and thus the sacrifices he must make to fulfill his promises. The reader, then, is forced to read the poem symbolically, whether he is conscious of doing so or not.

Yet when one examines it, one is at a loss to say just how Frost's images direct the reader's mind to this broader area of meaning. Austin Warren has attempted to solve the problem by suggesting that Frost uses a "natural symbolism." [3] Sleep by its very nature suggests death; so does darkness; and snow too, because of its association with winter and the danger of freezing. Likewise, woods are a familiar archetypal image for perilous enchantment. There is some value in Warren's theory, but I do not think it will carry us very far. True, Frost could not use sleep to suggest death if there were not something intrinsically deathlike in sleep; you cannot make the snail a symbol of speed. But the symbolic meaning of even the most "natural" symbols is not fixed. In poetry, sleep does not always represent

3. René Wellek and Austin Warren, "Image, Metaphor, Symbol, Myth," *Theory of Literature* (New York, 1949), pp. 194–5. Warren's authorship of this chapter is indicated in the preface, p. vi.

death; it may refer to something else or have no symbolic meaning at all. The fact is that things in themselves have only a potential meaning, and this potential is very broad, very indefinite. Doubtless there are limits to what any one thing can suggest, but the possibilities are manifold, and what it does mean in any particular poem will depend on how the poet uses it.

To some extent Frost's symbols define each other. For example, the woods the poet enjoys looking upon are opposed to the promises he must keep, and it is clear that they represent a kind of irresponsibility. Again, since the poet will allow himself to sleep only after he has kept his promises, sleep becomes a *deserved* reward in contrast to the *unearned* pleasure of looking at the woods. But however carefully one studies the relations between the symbols one cannot find in them any explanation of how they are made to point beyond the particular experience described toward the far more fundamental realities of the speaker's and every man's life. Why does sleep in this context symbolize death? Why do the promises include so much more than the simple tasks which will not get done if the poet lingers too long at the roadside? And above all, why does the poet's experience come to represent a conflict present in all human life?

These are questions which anyone seriously interested in the structure of Frost's verse will have to confront. To answer them we must turn away from the symbols themselves to another element, one so obvious that its function has been generally neglected. This is the rural context within which Frost's most characteristic poems are presented. Frost's ruralism has been recognized from the beginning, but commentators have tended to view it primarily as a source of subject matter. The rural world, however, is not only the area in which Frost finds his most congenial subjects; it provides the framework in terms of which he can most effectively picture reality. In other words, the rural world supplies not only the objects, the events, the characters he writes about, but also the point of view from which they are seen. In "Stopping by Woods," for example, the poet casts himself in the role of a rural character—a man riding home across the countryside in a horse-drawn sleigh—and we are made to see the incident the poem describes through his eyes. So natural does this perspective seem and so thoroughly appropriate to the subject that one may well be unaware of it; yet it is the rural point of view, I would suggest, which offers the key to the poet's technique.

Frost's mode of symbolic reference is of a special kind. It is one which does not work primarily through allusion, metaphor, allegory, or explicit comment, but grows, rather, from the special perspective which the poet adopts. By viewing reality from a carefully selected point of vantage, he is able to reveal what is closest to him and most particular in its universal aspect. In his characteristic poems this point of vantage is the rural world, and the poetic vision it reveals, pastoral.

The present essay is a study of Frost's pastoralism. The thesis which I shall argue is that the structure of his most representative and important work is essentially that of pastoral. No good poet writes by formula, and the variety of Frost's verse both in subject and technique should not be ignored. Not all of his poems are pastorals; indeed, I should say that only a minority belong within the genre. Nevertheless, there is at the center of his work a characteristic design which pastoralism most effectively defines. My objective will be, not to account for every aspect of his poetry, but to describe the pastoral mode, which has in varying degrees determined the form of his verse. His many nonpastoral poems will, I think, become more understandable when this is done, for we will then be able to see how several other important aspects of his writing are traceable to the central design of pastoral. The concept of pastoral reveals the unity in the diverse elements of Frost's art; it should also enable the reader to look beneath the simple surface of the poems and recognize the really difficult problems of interpretation to be found there.

The claim that Frost is a pastoral poet may not appear surprising to many readers, for since the beginning of his literary career commentators have spoken of his verse in terms of pastoralism. In an important early review Lascelles Abercrombie wrote:

> Poetry in Mr. Frost exhibits almost the identical desires and impulses we see in the "bucolic" poems of Theocritus. Nothing so futile as a comparison of personal talents is meant by this; but for general motives, the comparison is true and very suggestive. Poetry, in this book [North of Boston], seems determined, once more, just as it was in Alexandria, to invigorate itself by utilizing the traits and necessities of common life, the habits of common speech, the minds and hearts of common folk.[4]

The same idea has often been echoed by other writers, and it is now not unusual to hear Frost casually referred to as a pastoral poet and his poems likened to eclogues. But, unfortunately, no one has yet followed up Abercrombie's cogent observation. Pastoralism and related terms have been applied to Frost at random simply as convenient descriptive labels; no one has undertaken to examine the pastoral elements in his poetry or interpret the significance of the comparison. In the present study, I shall take the term pastoralism more seriously. It will be used to denote

4. Review of *North of Boston*, reprinted in *Recognition of Robert Frost*, ed. Richard Thornton (New York, Henry Holt, 1937), p. 28.

that mode of viewing common experience through the medium of the rural world which we have already noted in "Stopping by Woods." To understand the kind of poetry this special perspective makes possible, we must turn aside for the moment and consider the essential nature of pastoral.

The pastoral genre can best be defined as a particular synthesis of attitudes toward the rural world. One might call this a point of view. It is one not to be found in every age, and among poets, at least, it is rare today. However, pastoral has had its periods of vigorous growth—notably during the cultural ascendancy of Alexandria, the age of Virgil, and the Renaissance. We need not seek for elaborate social explanations. Pastoral comes to life whenever the poet is able to adopt its special point of view—whenever he casts himself in the role of the country dweller and writes about life in terms of the contrast between the rural world, with its rustic scenery and naive, humble folk, and the great outer world of the powerful, the wealthy, and the sophisticated. Though rural life is the subject of pastoral, it is not seen in and for itself: the poet always tends to view it with reference to the more sophisticated plane of experience upon which both he and his audience live. As W. W. Greg states the matter:

> What does appear to be a constant element in the pastoral as known to literature is the recognition of a contrast, implicit or expressed, between pastoral life and some more complex type of civilization. . . . Only when the shepherd-songs ceased to be the outcome of unalloyed pastoral conditions did they become distinctively pastoral. It is therefore significant that the earliest pastoral poetry with which we are acquainted, whatever half articulate experiments may

have preceded it, was itself directly born of the contrast between the recollections of a childhood spent among the Sicilian uplands and the crowded social and intellectual city-life of Alexandria.[5]

The purpose of pastoral is not simply to render a set appraisal of the country. The contrast between town and country is an ever-vital principle of poetic organization, for the relation between the two is felt to be complex. Though urban life is obviously superior in wealth and formalized knowledge, the country has its own special values. Pastoral plays the two against each other, exploiting the tension between their respective values, elaborating the ambiguity of feeling which results, and drawing attention to the resemblances beneath the obvious differences.

One well-known characteristic of pastoral, its tendency to idealize the rural world, must be understood in this light. It is normal in human nature to go along with the values of the town, to desire wealth, power, comfort, and all the other good things which only a highly developed city culture can give. But it is also natural to have misgivings about such desires. The pastoral poet expresses these misgivings, and in so doing teaches the lesson of humility. His professed purpose, though it is not his real one, is to show that the rude and humble is better than the high and mighty—that flower wreaths are more ennobling than diadems, the conversations of shepherds in a way wiser than the debates of counsellors, spontaneous feelings finer than social graces. In other words, he argues for the superiority of the country, and this can best be seen in the characteristic assumptions of pastoral. It assumes that in the rural world man is closer to reality and hence may be said to have a special folk wisdom born of simplicity. Since the rustic earns his living from the soil, he is independent of

5. *Pastoral Poetry and Pastoral Drama* (London, Bullen, 1906), pp. 4–5.

the complicated social structure of the urban world; he lives on a simplified plane where the fundamental facts of existence are to be found in their most natural and understandable form. Thus his every action as he goes about his daily work takes on a heightened significance. The manifold activities which in the town are divided among the different classes and varieties of men are combined in the life of the swain. He is the king of his flocks, the courtier who woos Pastorella and dances at the sheepshearing, the artist in his singing, the politician and philosopher of pastoral debates, and the peasant earning his bread through physical toil. Though the swain may not be master of his fate, he at least lives in a world where it is easily recognizable.

Furthermore, pastoral idealizes the swain in another way by emphasizing the purity of his life. Instead of seeking the luxuries and corrupt pleasures of the worldly man, he eats simple, healthy fare and amuses himself in rural games. The sophisticated are taken up with abstruse reasoning; the swain sees life directly with a fresh sincerity. Behind all this, of course, lies the idea of innocence. Pastoral tends to merge with the myth of the golden age, because it assumes that in the rural world life retains its pristine purity. The swain, untainted by the evils of civilization, is a sort of ideal man, like the noble savage—not that he can escape evil or is completely free from it himself, but he has not been exposed to the subtle corruptions of a complex society.

The idealizing of country life, however, is only one aspect of pastoral. The contrast between country and town involves a recognition of two sets of values, and pastoral does not simply eulogize the rural world at the expense of the great world beyond. To make the picture of rural life all good is to deprive it of its relevance to ordinary experience, with the result that it will be shallow and merely pretty—as indeed it becomes in the decadent pastoralism of the eighteenth century.[6] The pastoral poet's real power springs from his ability to keep the two worlds in equilibrium. While he gives us an idealized picture of the country, he must at the same time cultivate our awareness of the real values of the more sophisticated point of view. Thus pastoral is to be distinguished from primitive art. It is not the spontaneous overflow of peasant song, but quite the opposite. It is always the product of a very highly developed society and arises from the impulse to look back with yearning and a degree of nostalgia toward the simpler, purer life which such a society has left behind. William Empson, in his stimulating book, *English Pastoral Poetry,* defines pastoral very convincingly as a mode of reestablishing for the refined classes the sense of solidarity with the common folk. He writes:

> The essential trick of the old pastoral, which was felt to imply a beautiful relation between rich and poor, was to make simple people express strong feelings (felt as the most universal subject, something fundamentally true about everybody) in learned and fashionable language (so that you wrote about the best subject in the best way). From seeing the two sorts of people combined like this you thought better of both; the best parts of both were used. The effect was in some degree to combine in the reader or author the merits of the two sorts; he was made to mirror in himself more completely the effective elements of the society he lived in.[7]

A truly rustic poet could not manage a maneuver of this sort. His knowledge would be circumscribed by the bounds

6. The decay resulting from a pure idealizing of rural life without any counterbalancing recognition of the values of the sophisticated world is apparent in Pope's pastorals.

7. *English Pastoral Poetry* (New York, W. W. Norton, 1938), pp. 11-12.

of the rural community, and if the folk ballads which have come down to us are any evidence, he would not be much interested in idealizing his own world but would strive to look beyond it to the great world of wealth and heroic action. The pastoralist must of necessity be a man of sophistication writing for a sophisticated audience, for to yearn for the rustic life one must first know the great world from which it offers an escape. The pastoral refrain, "come away," must be taken, then, in a special sense. The poet may insist that it is desirable to be poor and humble or that one is better off without the advantages of city culture, but when he invites his audience to return to the innocent rural way of life this is hardly a call to action. It is rather an invitation to recognize that Arcadia manifests universal realities in the purest and simplest forms, and to measure the world one knows by this ideal world.

That Frost's dominant mode is pastoral may at first seem doubtful, because the conventions so characteristic of this genre are not to be found in his verse. The unhappy shepherd, the fair shepherdess, the wandering flock, the daisies and violets, the greensward dance, the flowery wreath and oaten pipe represent a cluster of motifs which can be traced in the tradition from Theocritus to Pope and beyond into the nineteenth century. So prominent are the conventions that one may suppose they are an essential element of pastoral form. Part of the pleasure which the old pastorals offer is that of recognizing the familiar images as they appear, just as another part consists in noting how skillfully the poet handles the traditional devices of dialogue, singing contest, and lament.

Frost stands outside of this tradition, and to understand his pastoralism we must recognize that the conventions, while typical of the genre, are not a necessary part of its poetic structure. Pastoralism, as the term is generally used, signifies two related but not identical things. It refers to a particular group of poems forming a distinct tradition and also to a kind of poetry possessing a certain fundamental form. The two meanings are inextricably bound together in the public mind, because it is assumed that only the works in line of descent from Theocritus are true instances of the genre. This identifying of the genre with the tradition results from the belief that the conventions are the very core of pastoral. A moment's reflection, however, will show us that this is not so. Consider the many poems which make use of the conventional machinery but are quite different from pastoral. Wordsworth's "Immortality Ode" and Arnold's "Thyrsis" are two clear instances. In the great ode Wordsworth does no more than suggest a parallel with pastoral, while his "Michael," which (beyond the protagonist's occupation as a shepherd) contains nothing conventional, is a genuine eclogue. The pastoral images of "Thyrsis" seem curios brought home from a literary excursion, and although Arnold often reverts to them as if by an effort of will, their main function is to serve as points of departure into lush passages of nature poetry. The conventions are not the true basis of pastoral, but an outgrowth of something deeper and more fundamental. Pastoralism requires an established myth of the rural world, and the conventions gradually developed through tradition belong to the myth of Arcadia. They are formalized symbols whose function is to evoke an imaginative vision of this world. But Arcadia is not the only version of rural life, and it is possible for a poet to write true pastorals within the context of some other mythic rural world.

Frost's reasons for working outside the framework of pastoral conventions may be best explained with reference to the decay of the Arcadian myth to which they belong. When Frost began to write, the pastoralism of tradition had long since gone—disappeared with a finality which de-

fied the most strenuous efforts of the nineteenth century
to revive it. By the early eighteenth century there had been
a marked change in prevailing attitudes toward rural
life, and one may note that the death of the old pastoral
closely coincides with the advent of modern science and
the humanitarianism it fostered. "Lycidas" is the last great
traditional eclogue in our language, yet even in this poem
the form seems on the point of dissolution, as if Milton
found he could make the conventions work only by
treating them in a skeptical and self-conscious way. Pope's
pastorals, written in his youth, represent the last attempt
which can be termed a success, and this but a partial one.
A generation later Dr. Johnson, in writing of "Lycidas,"
dismisses the genre as "easy, vulgar, and therefore disgust-
ing: whatever images it can supply, are long ago exhausted;
and its inherent improbability always forces dissatisfaction
on the mind." [8]

Johnson's view has persisted more or less unchanged to
the present day. Yet it seems hardly sound, since the myth
of Arcadia flourished for many centuries; it did not always
seem so factitious. Even now the eclogues of Spenser,
Drayton, Herrick, and Milton are admired, though it is
hard to say whether we would like a modern poem on
Arcadia. Johnson describes pastoral as both exhausted
and improbable, but it is, I think, the latter term that
affords the best explanation of what happened to the old
myth. For if the overfamiliarity of Arcadian poetry could
in itself have destroyed the effectiveness of pastoral the
genre would have lost its appeal long before it actually
did. The fact is that during the Renaissance, as during
the other great periods of the tradition, Arcadia seemed
true to the realities of rural life. While from an early
date it was admittedly a fiction, as the stylized conventions

8. "Milton," *Lives of the English Poets* (Oxford World's Classics), ed.
Arthur Waugh (London, 1955), *1*, 112.

indicate, nevertheless men had a certain faith in it. It was felt to represent a true picture of the country, if not in its particular details at least in its essentials; and so long as this faith persisted the poet was able to use the conventions as a medium for serious poetry. Indeed, in the best pastoral poetry the traditional materials are almost always reinvigorated by combination with a large measure of realism. The trick is to blend the conventional forms with the local details of one's own countryside. Thus Spenser has his shepherds speak in a pseudoarchaic language suggestive of regional dialect, while a like sense of realism is achieved by Shakespeare through the mixing of pastoralism and low life, as in Act IV, Scene 4 of *A Winter's Tale*. Similarly, Herrick in his pastoral lyrics combines the Arcadian imagery with a wealth of allusions to local customs and scenery.

The decline of pastoral resulted from the dwindling of belief in the old myth as a new attitude toward rustic life gradually took its place. With the emergence of a scientifically oriented mentality, the public began to take a more matter-of-fact view of rural conditions. Where the old pastoral had portrayed the rural world as an image of all levels of experience, there was now an increasing tendency to see the country in and for itself; and judged by the standards of literal truth, Arcadia could not but seem the shallowest of artifices. Hence Johnson's disgust at its improbability. Pastoralism persisted through the eighteenth century in popular art because of its appeal as a pretty, romantic legend, but one need not take its decadent stage too seriously. By this time the new interest in actual rural conditions had isolated the country and thereby destroyed the very spirit of the genre.[9] The

9. "The Deserted Village" illustrates the shift of interest very well. While it manifests the nostalgia and admiration for rural simplicity so important in pastoralism, the poem is one of social protest and focuses

shepherd swain had formerly been a symbol of human nature, but the actual peasant in his ignorance and bondage could not be, and the concept of the natural man was transferred to the primitive and the child.

The humanitarianism which grew up with the new science acted as another powerful dissolvent. The myth of Arcadia had assumed an unchanging social order and accepted the peasant's inferior status as natural and right; thus there is in pastoral an implicit fatalism quite contrary to the aspirations which the new thought raised.[1] As humanitarian ideals began to take hold, the old resignation was replaced by the hope of reform. The peasant's naïveté was seen as ignorance and his simple life as poverty. This led to pity and a kind of patronizing which made the pastoral attitude of admiration impossible.

In studying Frost's pastoralism we must recognize that it is an art which did not and could not have developed within the old framework.[2] As a matter of fact, one of

---

attention upon the actual state of the country in a way quite foreign to pastoral. Though the poet knows the village from his youth, he now looks at it from afar and directs the reader to do so also. The village is not a microcosm within which the world is mirrored, but a victim of the world to be pitied and, possibly, saved. Goldsmith's humanitarianism and his failure to use the traditional imagery of pastoral are both indicative of a quite different approach to rural life.

1. Empson makes this point very convincingly in his discussion of proletarian art. See *English Pastoral Poetry*, pp. 3–6 and 19–21.

2. It is true that Frost has on several occasions made use of the conventions of traditional pastoralism. The parallel between "Build Soil— A Political Pastoral" and Virgil's first eclogue and the probable influence of Virgil's eclogues upon Frost are treated in Chapter IV, p. 127. A little lyric reminiscent of the cavalier poets is entitled "The Peaceful Shepherd," and "Beech," which stands as the epigraph to *A Witness Tree*, is signed "The Moodie Forester," apparently in imitation of pastoral ballads of the Renaissance. On one occasion, Frost showed me a large, illustrated edition of Herrick, which he said was a favorite book of his during childhood. Here and there one suspects the influence of Herrick, especially in little poems about flowers such as "The Telephone."

Frost's earliest poems shows very clearly how remote the conventions of pastoral were from his own interest. In "Pan with Us" he uses the imagery of Arcadia to symbolize all the genteel poetic styles which were dying out during the period of his literary apprenticeship. In despair, Pan throws away his oaten pipes:

> They were pipes of pagan mirth,
> And the world had found new terms of worth.
> He laid him down on the sun-burned earth
>   And raveled a flower and looked away—
>   Play? Play?—What should he play?

The question posed in these lines is directly relevant to his own verse. If the pastoral tradition had long since lost its validity, how was he to write a poetry essentially pastoral? The answer to this question becomes apparent when one recalls the distinction between pastoralism as a kind of poetic structure and pastoralism in the narrower sense of a particular tradition. It was the tradition that had withered; the fundamental form remained as a potential. Occasionally this potential was realized, notably in the work of Burns, and in Wordsworth's "Michael" and a few of his short lyrics. Frost's achievement as a pastoral poet, like Burns' and Wordsworth's, is a distinctly individual triumph. It has resulted from his discovery of a new and realistic basis for examining the rural scene within the structure of pastoral.

To say this is to say that Frost discovered a new myth of rural life. When he wrote the lines quoted above he had not yet arrived at this; and I do not mean to suggest that the discovery was a conscious, reasoned one. As a poet Frost matured late; his early verse reveals a constant searching for an idiom and a subject. From the beginning his instincts drew him towards rural subjects, but in the long period of experiment we find him writing of these in an elegant manner reminiscent of late Victorian nature poetry. Only when he learned to adopt the perspective of pastoral and wrote from the point of view of an actual New England farmer did he come into his own as an artist. The change was a sudden one; it occurred when his imagination grasped the poetic possibilities of the region he knew so well, when, by leaving home for a brief sojourn in old England, he came to see in the life of rural New England a remote, ideal world which could serve the same function as Arcadia. The important role of regionalism in Frost's poetry is a large subject, and we will therefore have to explore his myth of New England more fully later on. For the moment, let us accept it as a myth. Our present purpose is to consider somewhat further the kind of poetry it makes possible.

Frost, like the writers of old pastoral, draws upon our feeling that the rural world is representative of human life in general. By working from this nodal idea he is able to develop in his poems a very broad range of reference without ever seeming to depart from particular matters of fact. He says nothing of other places and other times—he gives us only the minute particulars of his own immediate experience; yet, as we have seen in "Stopping by Woods," the things described seem everywhere to point beyond the rural world. The effect is to create a remarkable depth of reference. One senses a powerful symbolism at work in the poem, but when one attempts to specify just what the images refer to their meaning proves too delicate, too elusive to capture. One can define the poem's meaning in general terms, as I have done, but this is not entirely satisfactory. Such a definition can give only a flat, abstract statement of theme, whereas the beauty of such poetry consists in the presence of manifold particular references lurking behind the symbols.

A symbolism of this kind is neither defined by traditional references nor shaped through such devices as metaphor, but emerges, like the three dimensional effects of painting, from the very perspective of the poet's vision. Pastoralism, as we have noted, is characterized by a basic duality: it portrays rural life, but it always does this with reference to the great world beyond. Its essential technique is that of creating a sharp contrast between the two. The pastoral poet tends to emphasize the great distance which separates the shepherd from the aristocrat and the rustic setting from the city and court. His method is paradoxical in that his intent is to portray universal experience by revealing the basic realities common to both worlds, yet he achieves this by insisting upon their dissimilarity. If the country is to become the microcosm of the great world it must be pictured as a little world in itself, one which is separate from the realm of ordinary experience even though, in another sense, it displays the familiar reality. It is, then, by making his Arcadia remote that the pastoral poet transforms it into a symbolic world. And since the rustic scene in its entirety is taken as representative of all other levels of being, the things that belong to it—the shepherds and farmers, their tasks, amusements, and concerns, the simple objects familiar to them and the scenic aspects of their surroundings—are all infused with symbolic suggestions.

It is just such a perspective and such a method of pastoral contrast that gives the simple scenes and episodes Frost describes their extraordinary breadth of reference. When one considers his Yankee poems, one begins to notice a number of fundamental similarities between them and the old pastorals. His New England, like Arcadia, is a distinct plane of existence portrayed in such a way that a comparison with the outer world is always strongly implied. It is isolated from ordinary experience, a society with its own folkways, customs, and ideals, a locality with its own distinctive landscape. Like the old pastoralists, he emphasizes the uniqueness of his rural world. It is an agrarian society isolated within an urbanized world, and its country folk are separated from the modern reading public by a gulf of social, cultural, and economic differences nearly as broad as that dividing the swain of the old pastoral from the courtly reader. If the awareness of class differences, which is so prominent in traditional eclogues, is necessarily much less important in Frost's pastorals, regionalism provides another means for creating the effect of remoteness. He sets his rural world apart by stressing its distinctly local traits and portraying Yankee life as quite different from that in the cosmopolitan urban society. And as in the old pastoral, awareness of differences leads to a recognition of parallels. The more unusual and remote from everyday life his rural New England appears, the more effectively he can use it as a medium for the symbolic representation of realities in other areas of experience.[3]

Frost's method as pastoral poet is nicely illustrated by one of his most familiar lyrics, "The Pasture." This poem is of particular interest in that the poet has for many years used it as the epigraph for editions of his collected verse, a fact which suggests that he regards it as a symbol of the kind of poetry he writes. "The Pasture" may at first appear very simple indeed, since the materials of which it is composed are so slight. It seems merely to describe a few casual details of farm life which the poet sees in going about his tasks. But as in "Stopping by Woods," the bits of description somehow cohere to form a pattern which expresses a much broader meaning than is overtly stated.

3. Of course the remoteness cannot be too great. If the rural world were fantastic, like the fairylands of romance or the planets as depicted in science fiction, the particular kind of symbolism one finds in pastoral would not be possible. It should be remembered that the remoteness of the pastoral Arcadia is counterbalanced by its closeness to nature and hence to the physical reality underlying all life.

It is important to note that the poem is an invitation: the poet invites someone, perhaps a person he loves, perhaps just a friend, to come with him and see the glimpses of delicate beauty to be found in the pasture. The implication is that the person invited knows little of such things. More important, he will have to be initiated into the special way of looking at them which makes them precious and meaningful. The leaves floating in the pasture spring, the little calf, so young it totters when its mother licks it, have the simplicity and innocence of pristine reality, and the poem implies that the average person, like the person invited, could not see the beauty in such natural, everyday things without the poet as guide. To appreciate these, he will have to abandon knowledge as the great world understands it and learn to adopt the poet's special way of seeing.

The poet's invitation is really to a kind of vision, and this vision is to be understood through its implicit difference from the common view of reality. But the invitation is also to a place, the pasture itself, for only within the humble, out-of-the-way rural world is this special mode of perception possible. The pasture, then, is both the subject of the vision and its perspective; the mode of perception is embodied in the images themselves. For all its sweetness the poem is not tainted by sentimentality, because while it describes the charming aspects of the pasture, it is concerned less with beauty for its own sake than with the organic wholeness which makes this beauty meaningful. Frost's theme here is the coherence of the rural scene, the unity between the things observed and the way of seeing, between objects and thought, between man's work—the speaker of the poem must clean the spring and fetch the young calf—and his aesthetic experience. This unity raises the world of the pasture above other realms of human life by showing it as an ordered world where the significance of things is simple and apparent. This is manifest in the symbols themselves: the spring and the calf represent the source, the simple, pure, innocent beginnings of things.

Yet the special value of this world is paradoxical in that the pasture embodies a humble and naive level of being. The reader is to admire the pasture as a world better than his own because it is more natural, more neatly organized, and more meaningful, but he is also aware that it is a plane of existence inferior in many respects to that on which he lives. The contrast between the country and the town which we have noted in pastoral is clearly the essential element in the design of this poem. By making the rural scene remote from ordinary life and by implying that to understand it we must learn to adopt its special perspective, Frost establishes a comparison between the pasture and the outside world. It is from this implied comparison that the poem's elusive symbolism grows. The calf and the pasture spring emerge as symbols because they exist within a world which is viewed in its relation to other places and other modes of experience.

A symbolism created by the sustained contrast of pastoral has its being in the medium of analogy. This explains why in Frost's poetry metaphor is not a dominant element. Of course, Frost uses metaphor frequently and with great effect—at times, even, in a manner quite close to that of metaphysical poetry. But it is a device or figure of speech—it does not, as in Blake, Shelley, or Stevens, supply the essential pattern of thought; and this is so because the mode of thinking metaphor involves is different from that of pastoral. Metaphor establishes an identity between diverse things, while the pastoralist's technique is to keep the image and the thing it resembles separate so that they may be compared.[4] The result is that pastoralism favors an analogical form, a fact illustrated by its persistent tendency toward allegory—that is, extended analogy.

By taking the rural scene as a whole, a world complete in itself, and contrasting this with the great world, also seen as a whole, the pastoral poet divides experience into two distinct spheres. The division itself creates an awareness of the correspondences between the two. The poet need not give the things he describes a specific symbolic content, since the very framework of contrast within which they are presented brings out their universal aspect. Admittedly, the method could and often did degenerate into a contrived allegorizing such as one finds in portions of "The Shepheardes Calender." We must distinguish, however, between a flat and simple allegory which attaches labels to everything and the more normal allegorical form of pastoral. The best poems in the genre are not restricted in their symbolism to particular levels of reference; there may be many specific allusions, but these are only items within the more general areas of meaning toward which the pastoral images point. Even in "Lycidas" the allusions to contemporary religious controversy and the poet's own problems as an artist are actually rather obscure, and only the modern habit of reading the poem as a biographical document rather than a poem makes these levels of meaning seem the most important. The endless speculation as to what Milton meant by "that two-handed engine at the door" illustrates the futility of the effort to treat pastoral allegory as if its references were explicit. I have no doubt that Milton, when he wrote these words, had

4. Nowadays, there is a tendency to regard the difference between metaphor and simile as unimportant. Often metaphor is used to designate both. If we regard metaphor and simile merely as figures of speech the distinction may not seem important, but each represents a particular kind of poetic structure. In terms of an entire poem, the difference between metaphoric thought and that involved in simile is crucial.

some definite symbolic allusion in mind such as, for example, the two testaments; but in choosing to write a
pastoral, he adopted a poetic mode which works through
generalized symbols. The two-handed engine may represent the executioner's axe, the two houses of parliament,
and many other instruments of justice, since all such references come within the symbol's scope.

The broad and generalized symbolism characteristic of
pastoral results from the fact that the pastoral analogy is
implied, rather than stated. While the pastoral poet deals
with the great world as well as the rural, he does so indirectly. What he actually portrays is country life. The
area extending beyond the limits of his Arcadia serves as
a background against which the rural subject is seen in
clear silhouette; and precisely because this larger world
is never explicitly defined, the rustic scene can represent
many other levels of being. Such use of analogy makes
the difficulty of interpreting Frost's poetry understandable; it explains why his symbolism, though strongly felt,
is always hard to tie down to specific referents. The scenes
he portrays do not point toward particular things in other
contexts, but rather represent whole classes of experience
and types of things. We see this immediately when we attempt to specify what such images as the woods filled with
snow in "Stopping by Woods" or the newborn calf in
"The Pasture" symbolize. We can say that the woods represent a kind of temptation to indulge the imagination and
that the calf suggests birth, fertility, and natural innocence,
but beyond this one cannot safely go. In other words, we
can delimit the general area of meaning behind the symbol, but this area contains an indefinite number of referents, none of which can be chosen as *the* right one. Of
course, in all good poetry symbolic meaning will be manifold and ambiguous, but in Frost's it tends to be so broad
as to seem indefinite.

It is this, I believe, that accounts for a certain dissatisfaction which readers of modern poetry are apt to feel toward Frost's verse. The nature of his symbolism is such that the interpreter feels committed to extracting from his poems a general "message." He may be tempted to say, for instance, that "Stopping by Woods" expresses the idea that man must sacrifice his desire for pleasure and rest to his duty, loyalty to duty being essential to life, whereas the surrender to desire means death. Such general statements of meaning, however, will always appear too pat, and a poem which seems to call for them, suspect. This is especially so today, for modern poetry represents a reaction from the overt statement of ideas characteristic of nineteenth century verse. We distrust general ideas in poetry and are apt to condemn them as empty abstractions. The Imagist Manifesto, though long since found inadequate by the more important poets, expresses assumptions which still are widely accepted. The values which the prevailing taste tends to emphasize are concreteness, distinctness, particularity, and such taste will naturally prefer a symbolism in which the reference is definite. The recent popularity of Donne is indicative, for Donne's appeal to modern poets and readers seems to consist in the fact that in the metaphysical conceit not only the image but its referents are made explicit.

Frost's imagery is certainly no less distinct and particular than that of other contemporary poets, but the implied analogy of pastoral through which he works does not create a symbolism as precise in its reference as that of more typical modern poetry. In Eliot's "Sweeney Among the Nightingales," for example, one finds a use of symbols quite different from that we have noted in "The Pasture." Eliot's poem, like Frost's, is based upon the analogy between two distinct levels of being, but here both are stated. Sweeney and his milieu, the bordello or cheap eating

house where the hero finds himself surrounded by prostitutes and rather dangerous low-life criminals, comprise
the main subject, but its meaning is revealed by comparison with Agamemnon and the whole context of the house
of Atreus myth. The elements of Sweeney's story have
specific reference to the elements of the myth, Sweeney
to Agamemnon, the prostitutes who conspire against him
to Clytemnestra, and so forth. Of course, the meaning of
Eliot's symbols extends beyond these mythic parallels, but
nevertheless the symbolism has a quality of exactitude because the two levels compared are both presented. Frost,
by leaving one side of his analogy to implication, achieves
a symbolism which appears to be far less precise.

His poetry, however, has its own kind of precision.
While the referents of his symbols are not specified, the
area within which referents are to be found is strictly
delimited. While in Eliot the symbol most often has some
terminus (though this may be very distant indeed from
the symbol itself), and the meaning vibrates between the
two like an electric current between two poles, in Frost the
symbol, presented quite casually as an image, opens outward upon a vista of meaning. The vista does not have
any definite terminus and in the farthest distance fades
into vague areas of suggestion. What is definite is the *line*
of vision, the direction.

In "Mending Wall," for example, the difficulties raised
by Frost's mode of symbolism are apparent. The poem
seems merely descriptive and anecdotal in character, yet
everyone who has read it will remember a certain feeling
of puzzlement, a sense that Frost is driving at some point
which one is not quite able to grasp. We are told how the
speaker in the poem and his neighbor get together every
spring to repair the stone wall between their properties.
The neighbor, a crusty New England farmer, seems to
have a deep-seated faith in the value of walls. He declines

to explain his belief and will only reiterate his father's saying, "Good fences make good neighbors." The speaker is of the opposite opinion. As he points out:

> There where it is we do not need the wall:
> He is all pine and I am apple orchard.

To him the neighbor's adherence to his father's saying suggests the narrowness and blind habit of the primitive:

> He moves in darkness as it seems to me,
> Not of woods only and the shade of trees.

Yet the speaker's own attitude is also enigmatic and in some respects primitive. He seems to be in sympathy with some elemental spirit in nature which denies all boundaries:

> Something there is that doesn't love a wall,
> That sends the frozen-ground-swell under it,
> And spills the upper boulders in the sun;
> And makes gaps even two can pass abreast. . . .
>
> No one has seen them made or heard them made,
> But at spring mending-time we find them there. . . .
>
> Something there is that doesn't love a wall,
> That wants it down. I could say 'Elves' to him,
> But it's not elves exactly, and I'd rather
> He said it for himself.

The poem portrays a clash between these two points of view, and it may therefore seem that its meaning is the solution Frost offers to the disagreement. The poem leads one to ask, which is right, the speaker or his Yankee neighbor? Should man tear down the barriers which isolate individuals from one another, or should he recognize that distinctions and limits are necessary to human life? Frost does not really provide an answer, and the attempt to wrest one from his casual details and enigmatic comments would falsify his meaning. It is not Frost's purpose to convey a message or give us a pat lesson in human relations. Though the poem presents the speaker's attitude more sympathetically than the neighbor's, it does not offer this as the total meaning. Frost's intent is to portray a problem and explore the many different and paradoxical issues it involves. He pictures it within an incident from rural life, and in order to reveal its complex nature he develops it through the conflict of two opposed points of view. The clash between the speaker and his neighbor lays bare the issue, which within their world is the simple matter of whether or not it is worthwhile to maintain the unnecessary wall in defiance of nature's persistent attempt to tear it down. But one cannot avoid looking at this problem in other contexts of experience. The wall becomes the symbol for all kinds of man-made barriers. The two views of it represent general attitudes towards life—the one, a surrender to the natural forces which draw human beings together, the other, the conservatism which persists in keeping up the distinctions separating them.

It is tempting to make the symbolic meaning more specific, and there has in fact been a good deal of speculation about just what the wall represents. Does it signify class divisions, the barriers of racial prejudice, the misunderstanding between nations, or differences of religion? Similarly, the opposed opinions of the speaker and the old farmer seem to invite a comparison with political, philosophical, and ethical positions. One might see the poem as a contrast between the liberal and the conservative, the instinctualist and the rationalist, the man of charity and the man of justice. However, common sense tells us that the search for a single set of symbolic referents is futile. The evidence is lacking, and what is more important, such interpretation cannot account for the broad range of symbolic meaning which gives the poem its beauty and interest.

At the same time it would be equally foolish to pretend that the poem is just about the problem of mending a pasture wall. The interpretations suggested above should not be dismissed too scornfully, for while none taken by itself is adequate, all are within the scope of the poem's meaning. That the symbolism of "Mending Wall" in general does not mean that it is indefinite. While it lacks the specific kind of reference we have observed in Eliot's poem, it is clear and precise in a different way. Frost has exactly defined the nature of the problem he portrays, so that it represents, not vague classes of experience, but only other problems of the same kind. Though one may see in "Mending Wall" allusions to specific things outside the poem, even reminiscences of one's own past experience, their meanings will always have a certain fundamental similarity.

The comparison made earlier between Frost's mode of reference and the landscape vista indicates the kind of symbolism most characteristic of his work. Just as the vista delimits the observer's vision, Frost's symbols control the direction of the reader's thought; and although the path of reference may contain specific referents as the vista does objects, these are less interesting in themselves than the total view with its depth and the sense it creates of innumerable remote things related to the viewer's point of vantage. This conception should be helpful to the interpretation of Frost's poems. For one thing, it should save readers from the despairing view that, because his symbolic references are not specific, his poems lack any symbolic import and are to be taken merely as descriptions of particular places and personal experiences. Then,

too, it should serve as a guard against the opposite absurdity, that of reading Frost's poems as if they were
cryptograms in which every image has some set equivalent.
By thinking of Frost's symbolic reference as a vista rather
than an arrow moving from image to referent, one can
recognize specific references and yet see them in their
proper perspective as particular meanings within the scope
of a more general meaning. In "Mending Wall," for example, the wall does suggest other kinds of barriers, the
divisions between nations, classes, economic, racial, and
religious groups and the like, but no one of these or combination of them all exhausts the symbol's meaning. Nevertheless they fall within the range of reference; to recognize
their relevance is not to "read into" the poem, but to discover some small portion of what is actually there.

This view should demonstrate the need to scrutinize
the symbolism of Frost's poetry. Even when the poet seems
most determined to do no more than describe a scene
or episode, his imagery has a significance which extends
outward to range upon range of meaning. In " 'Out,
Out—,' " for example, he tells the story of how a boy loses
his hand by accident while cutting wood at a buzz saw
and dies only a few hours after. The effect of pathos is so
intense that one may at first suppose that this constitutes
the poem's main value. But sad events do not in themselves create moving poetry. Though Frost may seem only
to describe, actually he has so managed his description that
the boy's story symbolizes realities present everywhere in
the human situation. The key to the poem's meaning is
to be found in the fact that the loss of the hand causes almost immediate death:

> But the hand!
> The boy's first outcry was a rueful laugh,
> As he swung toward them holding up the hand

> Half in appeal, but half as if to keep
> The life from spilling. Then the boy saw all—
> Since he was old enough to know, big boy
> Doing a man's work, though a child at heart—
> He saw all spoiled.

Ordinarily an accident of this sort would not be mortal, especially when, as in this case, modern medical attention is within reach. "The doctor put him in the dark of ether," and there is no *physical* reason why he should not have recovered. His death is caused, rather, by his recognition of what the loss of a hand signifies in terms of his life: "the boy saw all— . . . He saw all spoiled." At the end

> They listened at his heart.
> Little—less—nothing!—and that ended it.
> No more to build on there.

The "all" that the boy sees is the complete and irretrievable ruin of his life. Any merely medical explanation of his death is irrelevant. He does not die of shock or a too intense sorrow but of his realization of the truth. It cannot be a matter of enduring great pain for a time or of learning to get along as a cripple. There is no choice; he *must* die, and the reader will understand the poem to the extent that he sees why this is so.

All is spoiled because of the very nature of the world in which the boy lives. The long opening description has the important function of defining this world. It is, of course, the rural world, the scene of the accident being the farmyard where the boy, along with others, is cutting firewood. Frost pictures the setting as a sort of rustic amphitheatre with the snarling saw at its center and, extending away in the distance,

> Five mountain ranges one behind the other
> Under the sunset far into Vermont.

One should also note that the boy is working, not just playing at work as children elsewhere might, and that the work is expected of him. This emphasizes the fact that in his world a man's livelihood, even at an early age, depends upon hard physical labor. For him, then, the loss of the hand means not only a painful abnormality, but perhaps even the loss of his ability to survive. The sexual symbolism of the hand which psychology has made familiar is relevant here; but other associations are still more important. In every context the hand is associated with power and creativity; in the boy's world, however, it is not just a symbol of these things, it is quite literally the instrument. The boy sees that in losing his hand he has lost the possibility of ever becoming fully a man, not only in the sense of being masculine, but in the sense of achieving the completeness of his nature. The poem implies that anything less than this completeness involves such a maiming that the individual, in an essential way, dies.

Some readers may prefer to view the poem simply as an episode illustrating the way in which horror bursts through the peaceful and familiar surface of life. Certainly, the boy's first reaction is one of surprise, rather than pain. Yet his death is the ultimate fact, and this is defined by his recognition of what the accident means. We can, I think, avoid "reading into" the poem by keeping in mind the fact that the boy's understanding is not a reasoned one, but comes in a flash of intuition. It is, one might say, a complete realization. And its completeness emphasizes the nature of the pastoral world: one gets the impression that only in such a world is the boy's intuitive recognition possible.

The title, of course, is taken from Macbeth's soliloquy upon learning of his wife's suicide, and there is some value in comparing the view of death presented in the poem with Macbeth's. As everyone will remember, the soliloquy describes life as meaningless, "a tale/ Told by an idiot, full of sound and fury,/ signifying nothing." Macbeth, because he refuses to recognize that guilt has caused his wife's death, as it will soon cause his own, cannot see the pattern which makes sense of events. Hence for him death also becomes meaningless, a trifling occurrence, like the going out of a candle. Yet despite his professed indifference to death Macbeth clings to his faith in the witches' prophecies and fights on, even when all hope is lost. The boy seems to accept death with the same resignation as that expressed in Macbeth's lines, and in some ways the poem reflects the meaninglessness Macbeth describes. True, the loss of the hand is purely accidental; there is no particular reason in nature why it had to happen. But the ironic contrast between the boy's story and the soliloquy is more important than their similarity. For the boy, unlike Macbeth, "sees all," and he therefore does not struggle to live. Furthermore, his death is meaningful, since it defines his life. Both the boy and the reader see why it must be, whereas Macbeth cannot see the significance of death.[5]

The comparison Frost invites us to make between the boy's story and Macbeth's illustrates the way the poem implies a commentary upon life as it is lived in areas far beyond the boy's humble world. Macbeth, after all, belongs to a world of heroic action and high politics, and the fact that he appears to be less wise than the boy shows us how the poet uses the contrast of pastoral to measure this exalted sphere by the standards of the simple scene he describes. The same process of measurement can be

5. Since writing this, I have found a discussion of the role of the Macbeth soliloquy in " 'Out, Out—' " in Laurence Perrine, *Sound and Sense: An Introduction to Poetry* (New York, 1956), pp. 108–9. Perrine points out the similarity between Macbeth's situation and that of the boy, but does not notice the vital difference the comparison uncovers, something perhaps not too important for his purpose, which is merely to show the effectiveness of literary allusions in poetry.

applied to other areas of meaning. For example, the poem leads one to raise the question as to whether life in modern urban society is not inferior to that of the boy's world. In the city, an injury such as the boy suffers would be curable and the victim would go on living, but that is so because the city represents a way of life in which man's physical being is not in such complete harmony with other aspects of his nature. The boy's death symbolizes not only a superior wisdom but a superior kind of existence, one in which there is a perfect coherence and order. The mind and body are unified, man's thought is manifested in physical action, and as we see in Frost's description of the sawdust—"Sweet-scented stuff when the breeze drew across it"—pleasure springs from natural, everyday things. The order and coherence make experience understandable, not only to the boy, who recognizes the truth so fully, but to the speaker, whose tone implies a clear grasp of the tragedy, and to those close to the boy: "And they, since they/ Were not the one dead, turned to their affairs." This is not indifference, but a frank acceptance of reality, such an acceptance as would only be possible in a world so perfectly coherent that the truth is plain.

However, the poem also reveals the limitations of the boy's world and makes us aware of the ways in which the great world is superior. The death, after all, is a bitter thing; there is much to be said for a world in which one can survive an accident such as the boy's. Ironically, it is the very advantages of the rural world that make it, in other ways, inferior: the boy's conception of life is such that any impairment is fatal; and the rural world is so perfectly organized that any disruption of the natural order may lead to catastrophe.

So far I have stressed the differences the poem implies between the rural world and other levels of being, but here, as elsewhere in pastoral, the similarities are at least as important. The saw and the amputated hand are both richly symbolic. The saw, while only a machine, seems almost to possess a will and feelings of its own. It "snarled" as it cut the wood, and at the moment of the accident "Leaped out at the boy's hand, or seemed to leap." Yet its sinister aspect results from its lack of intent or feeling; it is dangerous because it is merely mechanical. The contrast between the machine and human nature is central. The boy loses his hand for the very reason that he has emotions, desires, and purposes beyond the saw's simple function of cutting wood. He is hurt because he turns away happily when he hears it is time for supper. The saw may have cut the hand "As if to prove saws knew what supper meant," but, of course, it didn't know or care. The hand, as I have said, suggests all man's faculties of strength and creativity; the saw comes to stand for all the mechanisms by means of which he works, from the simplest farm implement to the most complex economic institutions. Frost's story, then, deals with a good deal more than the boy's personal misfortune. It symbolizes a tragic aspect of the human situation: the fact that man's economic means, for the very reason that they are mechanical in nature, can destroy him. The death may not always be a physical one, as in the boy's case, but a destruction of man's essential humanity.

"An Old Man's Winter Night" provides another good illustration of Frost's method. The poem is one of his finest, yet it has received very little attention, a fact which suggests that his way of molding description for symbolic purposes is not clearly recognized. He depicts an old man alone in his farmhouse on a winter night. The pathos of the portrait arises from the old man's lack of awareness. We see him first standing alone in a "creaking room," unable to see out of the windows, unable to remember why

he has come there. The imagery emphasizes the very narrow limits of his thought: while "All out-of-doors looked
darkly in at him," he could not see beyond the frosted
panes because of the lamp in his hand. The light imagery
is important, for it symbolizes consciousness, a consciousness which in his case is fading out in a weak, lonely, and
purposeless old age:

> A light he was to no one but himself
> Where now he sat, concerned with he knew what,
> A quiet light, and then not even that.

The inner light goes out as he falls asleep, and all that
remains is the concealed light of the wood stove and the
pale moonlight outside. This faint illumination emphasizes the old man's torpor as he lives on almost unaware,
without kindred or reason for living. In the description of
him asleep, the poet depicts his condition as a living death
in which the simple processes of physical life continue to
function in an automatic way long after the consciousness
which makes for real life has faded out:

> The log that shifted with a jolt
> Once in the stove, disturbed him and he shifted,
> And eased his heavy breathing, but still slept.

His loss of life, then, is a loss of awareness. Frost makes
this clear at the very end of the poem when he explains
what the old man's failure involves:

> One aged man—one man—can't keep a house,
> A farm, a countryside, or if he can,
> It's thus he does it of a winter night.

The word "keep" is ambiguous: to keep a house and a
farm, of course, usually means to do necessary physical
work; but to keep a countryside? Does it mean to keep
watch over the countryside, and if so what kind of watch,

for what purposes, against what dangers? An earlier passage will help to clarify the problem, for there also Frost alludes to the obscure duty which the man's old age forces him to give up:

> He consigned to the moon, such as she was,
> So late-arising, to the broken moon
> As better than the sun in any case
> For such a charge, his snow upon the roof,
> His icicles along the wall to keep.

They are, we see, *his* snow and *his* icicles, and if he can no longer "keep" them, the moon can. What is meant can best be understood with reference to the link between light and consciousness. The great danger threatening man's world—his house, his farm, his countryside—is chaos, the lack of meaning and lack of order represented here by darkness. We see this in the opening line, where the man, all alone in the empty room, is threatened by the sinister night beyond the window pane. The threat of danger appears to be in nature, but actually it is in man himself:

> And having scared the cellar under him
> In clomping here, he scared it once again
> In clomping off;—and scared the outer night,
> Which has its sounds, familiar, like the roar
> Of trees and crack of branches, common things,
> But nothing so like beating on a box.

The sounds in nature are "common things" portending no danger so great as the horror of meaninglessness in human experience when the mind loses its grasp of reality.

The poem, then, is not just a portrait of old age, but a definition of death itself. Through Frost's blending of old age, night, and winter we see death as a disappearance of order and meaning. One might conclude that order and

meaning in the external world depend upon the organizing power of the mind, and this is one important strand
of thought. But the total meaning is more complex than
this, for Frost also implies that these is a similar organizing power in nature. When the old man can no longer
"keep" his house, farm, and countryside, these are kept
by the moon. There are two kinds of order, the human
and the natural; when the first fails the second, at least,
will save the world from chaos. Furthermore, if the moon
can assume the powers of the mind, there must be an essential affinity between the two kinds of order. The poem
may emphasize the pathos of old age and the horror of
death, but it also implies a faith that though death always
seems to threaten universal annihilation, order, meaning,
and therefore life itself cannot really be destroyed.

The moon is perhaps the most vital symbol in the poem.
We have already noted its place in a whole series of light
images which represent consciousness, but it can be given
more specific definition. We learn that the moon is "better
than the sun in any case/ For such a charge." The contrast
does much to reveal the nature of the function it inherits
from the old man. It represents not the thoughts of the
day, active and practical, but those of reflection (if I may
exploit a familiar pun). It is primarily a symbol of the
imagination, that special power by which the old man, if
he were able, would "keep" his countryside. Of course,
Frost is here drawing upon the moon's traditional associations with love, mutability, dreams, magic, and art, but
these are seen as qualities of the imagination. It is bene-
ficent in that it keeps the darkness at bay; it works
through dreams and art; it has the mysterious power of
magic; and it suffers change yet transcends it as the moon
does in its cycle. Furthermore, imagination is a subtle
power working indirectly, as the moon sheds a faint reflected light. The moon, then, symbolizes the organizing

power in humanity and nature, a power which dies for the individual when his consciousness fades but which cannot itself die, because, though it controls and exists within the physical, it is a principle. This accounts for the richness in Frost's portrayal of the old man. His loneliness, dimmed thought, and nearness to death are all touchingly presented, yet at the same time the poem creates a feeling of acceptance. One senses that his condition, for all its pathos, is somehow natural, inevitable, and right. Such acceptance makes possible emotional effects of a very complex kind, as one can see by noting how Frost has brought more than a little humor into the poem without jeopardizing its predominant sadness:

> A light he was to no one but himself
> Where now he sat, concerned with he knew what,
> A quiet light, and then not even that.

These lines bear repeating, for they illustrate very well what subtle shades of feeling are produced by the speaker's frank recognition of reality, one which is neither bitter nor indifferent, but submissive to the harsh facts. If the old man is to be laughed at as well as pitied, the humor is of a thoughtful kind and arises from a realization that a light once so powerful could now be so dim.

Though the poem contains no references to things beyond the immediate scene such as the allusion to Macbeth's soliloquy in " 'Out, Out—,' " the symbolism here is of the same kind as we have observed in the other poems considered. One might say that Frost's portrayal of the old man implies a general definition of old age and death, and this is true. But the rays of symbolic suggestion extend beyond these subjects to illuminate other aspects of experience. As we have seen, the main theme is the relation between consciousness and life, or, to put it another way, between the imaginative power of the mind and the order without which there could be no reality. The portrait of the old man alone on a winter night symbolizes not only age and death, but any situation in which man's ability to keep watch upon his world seems about to fail. The reader is again referred to the final lines: the rich suggestiveness of the language illustrates the way Frost directs the reader's mind outward from the scene described toward other contexts:

> One aged man—one man—can't keep a house,
> A farm, a countryside, or if he can,
> It's thus he does it of a winter night.

The house and farm, when combined with the countryside, take on a very wide significance. The farmstead, like the house in which Eliot pictures Gerontion, suggests human institutions, society as a whole, and even an entire culture; and the countryside of the old man, the nation, and beyond this, the world.

While Frost's pastoral mode does not require an overt symbolism, the fact that explicit references do appear more than a few times indicates that this symbolism is present even when it is less apparent. In "The Onset," one finds a descriptive writing very like that of "An Old Man's Winter Night," yet here Frost uses several explicit symbols. The poem describes the poet's feelings at the onset of winter when the snow, which will cover his New England countryside until the spring thaw, first begins to come down. He knows that winter will be gone in time, but when it begins he always feels the finality of annihilation, as if the world could never again recover from the death of the year. His despair is compared to that of a man at death, who at last

> Gives up his errand, and lets death descend
> Upon him where he is, with nothing done
> To evil, no important triumph won,
> More than if life had never been begun.

The snow becomes a symbol, not only of death, but of evil. Man can never overcome evil, and the descent of winter, like the coming of death, represents the futility of his efforts to do so. Or so it seems to the poet when he hears the first snow "hissing on the yet uncovered ground."

In the second stanza, however, he seems to argue that these moods of despair are not really justified. After all, "winter death has never tried/ The earth but it has failed," and spring will come again, bringing "the peeper's silver croak." Thus it may seem that Frost is merely restating the optimistic conclusion of Shelley's "Ode to the West Wind." Yet his tone is far less confident and joyous than Shelley's. Even at the end it retains a sombre quality, and the final lines, far from expressing firm assurance that life and the good will at last prevail, are strangely enigmatic. "If Winter comes, can Spring be far behind?" may be the most obvious theme of the poem, but it is by no means the whole of its meaning; Frost has qualified this optimism by recognizing that if life and the good cannot be completely overwhelmed by death and evil, neither can these latter two ever be driven from the world completely.

This idea, of course, is implicit in the analogy of the seasons. It is not mere captiousness to argue that if winter will be followed by spring, spring will eventually lead back to winter. The awareness that death and evil must persist is expressed through symbols which appear quite naturally in Frost's description of spring. The most striking of these is found in the comparison between the rill of melted snow "That flashes tail through last year's withered brake" and a disappearing snake. The transformation of the snow into a serpentine stream suggests the fact that evil, though it disappears from sight for a time, does not really leave the world. The reference to the Satan of Milton, who flees Eden but does not leave the world, should be apparent even to readers who are unaware of Frost's very frequent use of allusions to the Fall. If the symbolism here seems surprising, one should suspend judgment until he has considered the final lines:

> Nothing will be left white but here a birch,
> And there a clump of houses with a church.

This last bit of description is curiously emphatic. Its effectiveness cannot be explained wholly by its pictorial value, for Frost might have chosen any one of a number of other authentic items from the New England landscape. One feels that Frost gives us a perfect image, one which completes the poem without easy explanations on the one hand or irrelevance on the other. The obvious motive of his choice is the whiteness of the birch, the houses, and the church. As in "Design," he seems to be hinting at some mysterious connection between things having, more or less by accident, the same coloration. The last line brings us back to the human world, and thus, to some degree, has a reassuring effect consonant with the speaker's faith in spring; but the houses and the church are *white*—and thus linked, in some strange way, with snow, the major symbol of the evil and death the onset threatens. The association is disquieting. Apparently the triumph of spring is not complete.

Clearly Frost does not mean to imply that the human world is one of evil and death. Whiteness in itself is quite innocent and the poet does not speculate about the meaning of white as Ishmael does (though in two other poems, "Desert Places" and "Design," the influence of Melville's famous chapter seems likely). That the church and houses in New England hamlets are commonly white is a happy accident. It enables Frost to suggest a contrast of the sort which, as I will show in a later chapter, is habitual with him—that between the human world and nature. The winter whiteness comes and goes with the seasonal rhythm, but the buildings are permanently white. The little hamlet represents the stable human order which man has established against the flux of nature. The poet himself manifests a similar stability: he may feel despair every year when the onset of winter begins, but he knows that spring will come. Though nature moves rhythmically from life to death, from good to evil, man is able to see both as constantly present in reality. Man's consciousness raises him above the natural order. Yet Frost, as many of his poems show, refuses to claim more for man's spirit than the facts will justify. Man does go down in the defeat of death, the poet does suffer the same despair every winter. Man's power of transcendence is limited by his tie to physical reality. Indeed, it is through the conflict with nature that the human world is brought into being: the cluster of houses is created as a defense against the rigors of winter, and the church manifests man's effort to overcome sin and death. In other words, the human world is born from the recognition of the evil and death the onset symbolizes. Frost's neat pairing of the church with the white birch stresses the importance of this relation between the human and the natural.

The imagery of the final lines has a crucial symbolic function. The "clump of houses with a church" resolves the problem of the poem, not by any appeal to orthodox religion, but by representing the power of human consciousness. It suggests that the answer to the onset is not a simple faith that all will turn out right in the end, but the mind's power to see the whole of reality, to remember spring even when winter seems to threaten final defeat. Frost's optimism is made acceptable because it is shown to be reasonable: we see that it is part of a view which recognizes the persistence of both good and evil in experience.

Two of the symbols here are more explicit than those of the other poems discussed. The church is quite obviously to be taken as an institution as well as a building; and the snake, compared to the melted snow (which "hissed" when it first fell), has its traditional significance as a symbol of evil. Yet the symbolism of these images is not different in quality from that of images with a less explicit reference which we have noted earlier. True, the church refers to a particular religion, whereas the wall of "Mending Wall" represents a great many different kinds of barriers, but the former symbol is really no less broad in scope. In "The Onset" Christianity symbolizes human institutions of all sorts, and beyond this, whatever formulations man has created as a means of transcending death. Similarly, the snake, while it points directly to the serpent of Genesis, signifies the general concept of evil which identifies sin with death and recognizes it as an essential part of reality. That Frost's explicit symbols are generically the same as the more indirect ones found in such a poem as "Mending Wall" can be seen in another way, by noting that these too grow naturally and as if by accident from his description of a scene. The white church is not only a symbol but a characteristic item in the New England landscape; and though the snake alludes to evil it is also an apt descriptive image.

There is, however, a limit to the degree of explicit reference possible in pastoral, and when Frost passes beyond this he produces a kind of poetry which, though it may be related to pastoral, is really quite different. "Sitting by a Bush in Broad Sunlight" will illustrate, and a Chapter which began with "Stopping by Woods" may fittingly conclude with this poem. For while the parallel between the titles might be an accident, it invites a comparison of much value. Both poems present a scene as an analogy, and the difference between them is one of emphasis. In "Stopping by Woods" attention is focused on the scene itself. It is portrayed with great vividness, and the symbolism emerges from the bits of telling description. In "Sitting by a Bush," the scene is indicated only by the title and a few hints in the first stanza:

> When I spread out my hand here today,
> I catch no more than a ray
> To feel of between thumb and fingers;
> No lasting effect of it lingers.

The four quatrains which make up the rest of the poem do not describe the poet as he sits in the sun, his feelings or the things he sees about him. Rather they interpret what is said in the first stanza, and interpret it in general terms. As the sunlight does not penetrate the poet's fingers, so the spiritual fire no longer creates new life from "sun-smitten slime," so God no longer intervenes directly in the affairs of the world. All life derives from the "one intake of fire," the creation, all spirit from the one revelation. The bush by which the poet sits is, of course, the burning bush of Moses, but it does not burn now, for the one revelation has been given:

> God once spoke to people by name.
> The sun once imparted its flame.
> One impulse persists as our breath;
> The other persists as our faith.

Whereas in "Stopping by Woods" several analogies are implied, here there is but one, and it is stated, with the result that each image has a clear reference. Not that this poem is inferior; rather I would suggest that it represents another of Frost's poetic modes. Its values are those of metaphysical poetry—wit, sharpness, precision.[6] It is one of

6. The characteristic of this kind of poem is a stated analogy, usually between some homely experience and a theory taken from theology, physics, astronomy, or archaeology. The verse form tends to have a strong and very regular meter, short lines (usually of three or four feet), and clever rhymes. The distinction between these poems and the

several pieces which show the link between Frost and the tradition of Emerson and Emily Dickinson. But "Stopping by Woods" is more truly representative of his art. The indirect and subtly suggestive quality of its symbolism results from his preference for implication rather than explicit statement. He does not interpret the scene; he uses it as the medium through which to view reality. Here, as in the other poems most characteristic of his verse, the rural world holds the center of attention, and the things described become symbolic because the entire setting within which we see them implies an analogy to range upon range of other contexts. This explains why even the most important symbols seem so uncontrived and appear to be merely descriptive details. The wall of piled field stones, the farmhouse on a winter night, and the white, clapboard church are all typical parts of the New England landscape. Their richness and complexity of meaning result from Frost's total vision of the rural world.

---

pastorals is sometimes hard to make, for there are borderline cases. "The Road Not Taken," for example, presents an analogy rather more explicit than is usual in the pastorals, but it is not so precise as that of "Sitting By a Bush." Some of the best poems belonging to the witty type are: "I Will Sing You One-O," "The Aim Was Song," "To Earthward," "Canis Major," "A Missive Missile," and "All Revelation." The last is one of the most important poems for those who wish to study the poet's thought.

CHAPTER 2

NEW HAMPSHIRE AND ARCADIA: THE REGIONAL MYTH

Frost is best known to the public as the poet of New England. Like Faulkner, he stands forth as both the interpreter and the representative of his regional culture. It is therefore quite natural that his poetry has been most valued for the precision with which it portrays the rural world "north of Boston." There have been many fine studies of the poet's relation to his Yankee environment, and these have done much in helping readers to a more sensitive appreciation of his verse. Yet while this approach has its value, there is in it a dangerous tendency to overemphasize pure subject matter to the neglect of form. One can become so interested in the "reality" of Frost's New England or so concerned to see the local landscape as a reflection of the poet's own experience that one forgets to notice the art through which the regional world is presented. Of course, the reader will want to know something about the locality Frost describes, just as he will want to know something about the poet's life. But if he is interested in Frost's poetry rather than the region, he will need to go beyond a consideration of whether or not Frost's New England is an accurate picture of the real place. He will want to discover how the poet has recreated this region within the medium of language. More important, he will be interested to see how he uses New England as a means of revealing what is universal rather than merely local. In the end, Frost's rural world is interesting because it symbolizes the world we ourselves know. Our main concern must be to discover how he has shaped his world as an image of every man's experience.

The best approach, I think, will be to remind ourselves that Frost's world is not New England itself, but a portrayal of it. It is a representation created in words, just as a landscape, however "realistic" it may be, is not the scene itself but a design created in pigment upon canvas. An appreciation of such a poem as "After Apple-Picking" is no more dependent upon direct knowledge of New Hampshire farm life than actual acquaintance with the Provençal landscape is necessary to the enjoyment of a painting by Cézanne. Those who find this hard to believe would do well to recall that Frost's regional poetry was first acclaimed by English readers. The point may seem obvious, but it deserves emphasis here. Where a poet's characters and settings are fictitious, we accept them as inventions and do not attempt a direct reference to reality; where real persons and places are depicted, one tends to take the writer's art for granted, as if all that it involved were a tracing of established lines. *Sporus*—Lord Hervey—see *Memoirs of the Reign of George II;* Egdon Heath—Exmoor, of course: one would think that the art of Pope or Hardy was a very simple matter indeed. And so with Frost's regional poetry. We must recognize that though his characters and settings are less obviously invented than those of pure fiction, they are imaginative in the same degree.

Frost's creativeness is most apparent in his continual work of selection. He could not tell us everything about New England, even if he desired to do so. He is committed to choosing those few aspects of the place which will re-create it within the limits of his poems. Everything depends upon the choice, and this has been strict. Where are the industrial cities of Massachusetts and Connecticut, the Maine fishing villages, the tobacco farms along the Connecticut River, the cranberry bogs of Cape Cod? Where are the French Canadians, the Portuguese, the Irish, the shrewd Yankee business men? All these are a part of the real New England, as much a part as anything in Frost's poetry, yet somehow they do not appear. There are a few isolated exceptions. Baptiste, in "The Ax-Helve," is of Gallic extraction, "Sand Dunes" and one or two other poems may portray scenes along the northern New England coast; but whatever concessions must be made to the captious are so slight as to make little difference.

The reader will object that Frost does not claim to describe the *whole* of New England. His subject is the region north of Boston, and within that region, only the rural areas and farm villages. But to admit this is to recognize that his selection is by nature creative. He has taken one particular kind of locality to stand for New England as a whole, one particular kind of Yankee to stand for the essential character of the New England mind. Like all major artistic decisions, the choice, once made, seems simple, even inevitable, but anyone familiar with other regional poets—Whittier, James Russell Lowell, Edwin Arlington Robinson, and Robert P. Tristram Coffin are instructive examples—will see the highly imaginative nature of Frost's choice. Comparison with these other poets is especially helpful in showing his greater exclusiveness. While he seems more of a realist, his regional picture is actually far more stylized. He seems to discriminate by a stricter standard. He chooses, not simply what is real in the region, what is *there,* but what is to his mind the most essential, what is representative. The delimiting of rural New England is only the first step. Even within the area we still find the great mass of detail suppressed in favor of a few significant local traits. Now it should be clear that this process of representing the locality as a whole through a limited set of visual images and of portraying the culture and mentality of the region through a particular kind of character is really a mode of symbolism. What emerges from Frost's scrupulous selection is not reality itself, but a symbolic picture expressing the essence of that reality.

The title of this chapter is intended to suggest its thesis. I propose that we can best understand Frost's New England by thinking of it as a pastoral myth, a new version of Arcadia, which serves much the same purpose in his poetry as the old Arcadia in the eclogues of tradition. The term myth has been used so loosely in recent times that some explanation is needed as to just how it can be applied to Frost. Granted, we are not here dealing with myth in the sense of fable, but the concept is nevertheless useful. For what distinguishes myth is not its normally narrative content so much as the kind of imaginative response it assumes. I suppose it will be generally admitted that myth differs from descriptive accounts of reality in that its method is symbolic. The difference between myth and fiction is harder to grasp. It consists, I think, in the fact that myth enlists a far larger measure of literal belief. One might say that myths are fictions presented with such confidence that they seem to have the authority of facts. Considering the prominence of fantasy in the myths most familiar to us, this definition may at first seem very wide of the truth. But the myths we recognize as myths are, of course, those of alien or dead societies. For us, they cannot have a mythic status, because we do not share the beliefs upon which they are formed. This is really what we mean when we say that they are fantastic. There is a good deal of self-delusion in this. The concept of myth is currently enjoying great prestige: we admire myths as art and take them very seriously as a means by which a society formulates its experience, but this is not at all the same as viewing myth in the spirit of its originators. The value which we find in ancient and primitive myths is really the same value we find in fiction. If myth is considered the higher form, it is because we prefer the fictions supposed to have been produced by society as a whole to those of an individual artist. The idea of communal art is, for various reasons, very appealing to us, and behind this lurks the desire, emergent in Jung's writings, that through the study of myth we may be able to penetrate to the collective unconscious. However much myth is respected today, it is always strictly distinguished from literal truth. Thus, literary critics favor the sort of contrast which explains the value of myth by opposing it to "a scientific account." In anthropology the practice is to treat myths as data from which a society's history, political evolution, and technological advance may be abstracted. One translates the myths into practical terms, so that stories of the Daedalus variety, for example, are seen as records of the development of crafts.

No censure of this approach is intended. It is hard to imagine how we, within our own cultural context, could regard the myths of other peoples except as fictions. I would only point out that our attitude is very different from that in which the myths were first received. Indeed, nothing destroys the original response to a myth so effectively as the recognition of it *as a myth*. The true believer does not welcome a mythic explanation of his scriptures.

Of course, fiction enlists belief of a kind. In fiction characters, places, and events which are not in themselves real are used to represent things which are—the relations between events, the movement of thought in the mind, the action of the past upon the present, and so on. Now a myth is no less meaningful when it is viewed as fiction, and its aesthetic value may actually be more clearly seen in this way. The only thing lost is the sense of objective reality which it had for those to whom it was current truth. Even this is not destroyed for the sophisticated reader, but manifests itself in the qualities of spontaneity, naturalness, and profound insight which make myth seem somehow superior to conscious fiction. In other words, the essence of myth is its internal structure. We need not appeal to the beliefs of its maker or its original audience; these are just symptomatic. Myth should be understood in itself as a kind of art in which the imaginative symbols are presented as if they were literal facts.

If Frost's New England is hard to recognize as myth, it is largely because *as myth* it is still very much alive. This is illustrated by the literal-minded way in which his poems are commonly read. It is significant that Frost is hailed as the poet of humble facts, the straightforward realist who does no more than record the scenes and experiences he himself has encountered. This naive acceptance may seem to result from the fact that he writes of a real place, but there is much more to it than that. There are many ways of describing a place, yet his way seems to us the *right* one; that is, his choice of symbols appears so natural that we do not see it as symbolism at all. The things he pictures seem to us the most representative, and so the impression is created that the poet is merely describing. The reason is that his whole conception of New England is founded upon beliefs so unquestioningly accepted that the modern reader is scarcely aware of them.

We may see this by noting how unquestioningly the reader accepts Frost's premise that the real truth about a locality is to be found in its rural rather than its urban life. The basis of this assumption is the belief that man, in his natural and healthy state, is organically related to his environment, and therefore that human nature is purest

and most understandable where we find it in the most
direct and simple relation to its physical setting. Hence
regional poetry. The locality, we assume, shapes the man,
and the more the poet dwells upon its distinctly local aspects, both as these appear in the landscape and are reflected in the human character, the closer he comes to seeing the life-process itself. No doubt, a distrust of urban
life is as old as civilization. It has always provided a motive
for pastoral, and Frost's regionalism expresses this distrust
in its essentially modern form. Since the emergence of
Romanticism in the mid-eighteenth century, the idea that
urban society is artificial and therefore unnatural has been
a prominent part of the educated person's tacit belief. Because Frost draws upon the environmentalistic and primi-
tivistic tendencies in modern thought, his poems enlist the
literal acceptance of myth. He can represent New England
as a whole through the image of the Yankee farmer in his
rock-strewn pasture without seeming to go beyond objective description. For the contemporary audience, the rural
landscape and the farmer are the *real* New England, so that
we do not for a moment reflect that they are chosen from
a heterogeneous mass of other things equally real and
shaped by the poet's imagination as symbols of the whole.
The very way in which we take his stylized regional world
as New England itself shows the mythic status of this
vision.

When prevailing beliefs are modified, such a reading of
Frost will no longer be possible, but this does not mean
that his poems will come to seem less valuable. Readers
may actually have a better appreciation of them when their
imaginative nature becomes more apparent, just as we
may well have a finer response to old myths than the people for whom they were made. But at that time pastoralism
will take another form.

Naive literalism on the part of the audience is only a

symptom of myth; the evidence of the poems themselves is much more important. The mythic nature of Frost's New England can best be seen in its unity and stability. The region, as he depicts it, is not just a place; it is a world, coherent and complete within itself. This wholeness illustrates the difference between his art and that of lesser regional poets. At best, they portray a series of independent scenes observed from varying angles. Frost is able to describe some particular place, a sugar orchard, a brook in the woods, or a pasture and at the same time make us aware of the region as a whole stretching away on every side toward the horizon and beyond. We see only the maples, the brook, or the pasture, but we sense the presence of an entire locality inhabited by a particular breed of men who live in a certain way by certain lights. Very little in the way of factual statement is needed to accomplish this. Such short poems as "Hyla Brook" and "Desert Places" show that even within the space of a dozen lines or so he can create an image of the entire locality. Furthermore, the regional world seems exactly the same in poem after poem. The New England of "Mending Wall" is the same New England we find in "Birches"; the New England of "The Code" is the New England of "Stopping by Woods." "Home Burial," "The Star-Splitter," "An Old Man's Winter Night," "The Cow in Apple Time" all exist within a single world.

These aspects of Frost's art are striking. They suggest that there is a vital difference between his conception of New England and the fictional worlds we commonly find in literature. Of course, in any work where the setting is important it will tend to have a symbolic value or at least a special fitness to the subject. But when a poet uses the same setting again and again in poems written over a long period, and when he conceives it so completely that he can portray it as a whole through a few symbolic images, it takes on the character of myth. Such is the nature of Frost's New England. It is not just a scene of action or a rostrum from which to deliver lyric utterance, but an imaginative framework within which the poet's mind habitually moves. Like Blake and the mature Yeats, Frost is most effective when he writes in terms of a particular poetic vision. The fact that it is a vision of simple country life rather than an apocalyptic fable does not make it any the less a myth.

As readers, our main concern is to see how Frost has shaped this myth and to discover its function in his poetry. We may best begin, I think, by considering the nature of regionalism.[1] This is never a purely factual recording of local life. Its purpose, whether it deals with the Scottish highlands, the pioneering west, or any other exotic place, is to seek out local differences, and in emphasizing what is unique it always tends to distort reality, if not entirely to remake it. The motive appears to be a desire to recapture that old sense of connection between man and his physical environment which is lacking in a modern industrial society. Thus regionalism may be understood as a popular art which satisfies a vague but widely felt yearning to look back toward a simpler life. As nearly everyone has remarked, industrialization has tended to level the distinctions between places, and in this way it deprives the individual of the feeling that he belongs to a particular locality, or, as the cliché puts it, has roots. Also industrialism means specialization, and this destroys the coherence of experience, breaking it up into a number of unrelated activities. One result of this has been to foster a taste for

1. The only work known to me which deals with this subject effectively is Benjamin T. Spencer, "Regionalism in American Literature," in *Regionalism in America,* ed. Merrill Jensen (Madison, 1951), pp. 219–57. Spencer's essay is an historical summary of regionalism as a literary concept.

regional lore. The few areas which have escaped the blight have taken on the glamour of an idealized past and provide the materials for one kind of public daydream. The more everyday life is emptied of its local variety, the more eagerly people search for it in quaint, faraway places. One sees this again and again in a number of popular preferences—in the idea that a home should be built to suggest a Norman cottage or a colonial "salt box," in the notion that the vacationer should leave the "beaten path" and visit the fishing village or hill town where life seems somehow more genuine, in the taste for folk handicrafts. Now, of course, all this is not regionalism, but it indicates the synthesis of feelings from which regionalism develops.

The essential element in regionalism is the concern with local differences. Its basis is, therefore, a strong sense of contrast. Whether we consider it in the writer of regional fiction or just in the average man who has a vague liking for picturesque scenery, the thought process is the same. It is that of looking back toward the old ranch, the plantation, the farming village, or some other remote place with a constant awareness of the difference between that locality and the observer's own world.

Thus regionalism is always potentially pastoral. It establishes a comparison between the rural world, seen in terms of its richly picturesque local traits, and the complex industrial society of today, just as the old pastoral established a comparison between peasant life and the court. In both cases, the contrast involves a juxtaposing of past and present. The old pastoral associated Arcadia with the golden age, a state of primitive innocence in terms of which the audience could judge the more complicated and corrupt world of the present. For the aristocratic reader the comparison seemed natural, since in his own life he could compare a childhood at the family's country estate with his less happy adult life in court or city. Furthermore, one of the main themes both in Hellenic and Renaissance pastoral is sadness at the passing of the good old days when the nobility stayed home and attended to their land instead of rushing to court to waste their fortunes in dissipation or political intrigue. Regionalism exploits a similar historical contrast by looking back from a present of advanced technology to the period, still not very far away, when the roads were dirt lanes, farmers walked behind horse-drawn ploughs, and the rural community depended pretty much on its own produce. And in America, at least, this sense of historic change blends with recollections of childhood on the farm or in a small town.

The same fundamental contrast underlies both regionalism and pastoral, but regional art only becomes pastoral when the contrast is properly exploited. Not many writers have succeeded in turning local materials to the purpose of pastoral; Burns, Wordsworth, Hardy, and Faulkner are the most notable exceptions. The great bulk of regional writing is second or third rate, because it consists only in a sentimental picturing of local color. Instead of taking the contrast seriously, instead of projecting themselves into the local scene and viewing experience through the eyes of the swain, most regionalists look down from above—from Lowell's comfortable study, for instance— and from there local differences only seem charming, comic, and peculiar. Such writers are concerned merely with the difference between the local and the cosmopolitan, and this, in itself, has little interest or meaning.

Frost, on the other hand, does take the contrast at full value, because he has discovered what the local colorists missed, *that differences can be used as a means of revealing similarities.* He has learned that to make a picture of regional life true, in the deepest sense, one must not seek the unique traits of a place for their own sake, but must use these traits in such a way that they become symbols of what is universal. The aim is not to picture an unusual place, but to develop the image of the region as a world which somehow represents all other places. The basis of his achievement as a regional poet is this: that the very things which seem most unique to New England are the materials with which he suggests realities present on every level of experience.

The process is paradoxical. The more he emphasizes local differences, the more he isolates New England, sets it apart, as it were, from the rest of the universe. Yet it is this isolation which makes his New England symbolic. Only because it *is* set apart does the region cease to be merely a place, one of many places, and become a microcosm within which the great world beyond is mirrored. By constantly showing that the Yankee farmers who inhabit it think in a different and more subtle way, live by a different and more admirable ethic, Frost directs the reader's mind to compare this world with our own, to look for parallels, to see in the images presented veiled references to other things.

Clearly, the success of this method depends upon the poet's skill in discriminating. It is not just a matter of making the regional world as different as possible. Not every local trait, however typical, will serve his purposes. As a matter of fact, Frost has quite rightly rejected much of popular Yankee lore. Nothing would have been more damaging to his poetry than sentimentalized Christmas card scenery and the bric-a-brac of antique shops. The local materials must be so selected that they blend into a unified picture; they must seem to be parts of a single world.

There is, then, a high decorum controlling Frost's choice. This is something very elusive, since it is not based upon any set of conscious principles, but consists, rather, in a sense of fitness, a feeling on the poet's part for harmony between certain visual images, actions, traits of character, attitudes, and the voice tones that express them. Decorum is always hard to explain, but we can get some understanding of Frost's by noting two dominant ideas which seem to be constantly at the back of his mind. The first is that of a strong connection between the individual mind and the land itself. This is the aspect of his poetry which derives most directly from the Romantics. It is from them—most especially from Wordsworth—that he learned the technique of associating aspects of landscape and psychological traits. The clear, frank gaze of the Yankee *persona* is related to the chill air of New England and his strength of mind to its rugged terrain in the same subtle way that Michael's courage and dignity are related to the grandeur of the Lake Country mountains.

The second dominant idea is related to this. Since the Yankee mind reflects the landscape, the whole sense of values which forms the center of this mentality seems to have an organic relation to the land. This sense of values is present in every one of Frost's Yankee characters. It is something above their individuality, something which transcends personal traits while never veiling them. For lack of a better term, I shall call it a regional ethic. Nothing so simple as "morals" is meant. The regional ethic includes a code, but it also includes certain ways of thinking and a set of ideals which are more philosophic than moral—for example a special respect for the individual's rights, or particular attitudes towards work. To describe this ethic in terms of the familiar names for virtue— honesty, sincerity, industry, and the rest—is not helpful, since this only isolates the elements, whereas the ethic's validity and interest result from its inclusiveness, from the way it synthesizes the moral with the intellectual, the practical with the ideal, the human and psychological with the natural and physical. And this, after all, is one of the main objectives of Frost's regionalism. It presents values as an integral part of a way of life—not as abstractions, but as extensions into the mind of physical necessities.

I wish to emphasize again that the regional ethic is never a purely individual thing, and in this we can see a vital difference between Frost and Wordsworth. Although Wordsworth portrays a particular locality, his relation to it is individual. He is concerned with revealing the basic processes of the mind through a minute examination of his own experience, and it can be safely said that in his poetry there is only one fully developed character, that of the poet himself. Lucy, the old Cumberland beggar, the leech gatherer, Michael and the others are all seen at a distance as parts of the landscape. Where Wordsworth has tried for more complex characterization the failure is apparent. This may be compensated for by other values, but it does show how much his picturing of rural life differs from Frost's. For Frost's regionalism, like the old pastoral, is thoroughly social. It is concerned more with the rural way of life than with its scenery, more with the sense of values shared by the local society than with the intuitions of a single mind. Not that the community and the individual are opposed: the speaking voice in Frost's lyrics is certainly that of a particular person, but this person is also the spokesman for a community. Indeed, his identity depends upon his membership in it. This explains why Frost, unlike Wordsworth, can move easily from the lyric to the dramatic mode. The regional ethic, because it is shared, can serve as the basis for communication between characters as well as for the expression of personal emotion.

The way in which he has shaped New England as a pastoral myth is shown most clearly in "New Hampshire." This poem has been much neglected, perhaps because readers are put off by its discursiveness and seemingly loose structure. That it is discursive cannot be denied, for it pretends to be a specimen of chatty talk in which the poet rambles on at random from one to another of his favorite ideas. At first reading everything seems playfully irrelevant, and readers are apt to miss the underlying unity of the poem because they mistake the fictional pretense for the essential form. When a poet imitates conversation he will naturally avoid a clear line of argument. There is, however, an ordered progression in the poem. The form is much like that of Horace's epistles, and as in Horace, the details, though they seem to be introduced in a casual way, are actually woven together with great care.

The title of the poem suggests that it is a description of New Hampshire, and in a sense it is. But it is not, as no good poem can be, a full account of the place it describes. Those who expect a panoramic view are bound to be disappointed. What interests Frost is the essential spirit of the place, and thus in the end he portrays it as a point of view or mental state. Furthermore, since the speaker is the poet himself in fictional form, and since he takes on the role of regional spokesman, this mental state is identified with his own. There is a natural transition from description to self-explanation, from picturing the region to a defining of the poet's art. Ultimately the subject is Frost's own relation to the locality he writes of. The poem is therefore of great importance, for in it he gives us the fullest and most direct account of the place of regionalism in his poetry.

Since "New Hampshire" is a long poem, it will be convenient for the reader to begin by noting its general plan. It consists of four main sections, the divisions between them being marked by very clear turning points in the speaker's thought:

One could say in a general way that the first part defines the regional ethic, the second describes New Hampshire as a world in itself, the third evaluates this world as a subject for art, and the fourth illustrates how it serves the poet as a means of dealing with reality.

The poem begins in such a humorous way that the reader is likely to be disarmed and thus miss the essential contrast established here, which, as the poem modulates to more serious themes, becomes a vital part of its meaning. Frost starts by arguing the thesis that only in New Hampshire do people take a reasonable view of wealth. Through sketching a few rather absurd people he has met, he develops a sense of the difference between the New Hampshire point of view and that of other states—and by extension, of the outside world as a whole. His method is one of broad caricature. He tells us of a lady from the South who is actually proud that her family has never worked. She is compared with a man from Arkansas who bores the poet on a Pullman by boasting of his state's productivity. Then Frost cites a Californian who makes fantastic claims for California climate. And last he describes the poet from another state whose "fluid inspiration" has been degraded to "the best style of bad salesmanship" by his desire to defeat the Volstead Act. All of these people (even the southern lady in her genteel disgust) demonstrate the moral degradation of trade. "The having anything to sell is what/ Is the disgrace in man or state or nation," because, by New Hampshire standards, selling symbolizes a lack of self-sufficiency. This anecdotal humor sets the right tone for a conversational poem and enables the poet to approach his more serious ideas in an unassuming way.

New Hampshire, as everyone knows, is a poor state without natural resources, economic power, or political influence, so that Frost must somehow circumvent the danger—and it is a real one for every regionalist—that his humble subject will seem only humble and so dispose the reader to take a patronizing attitude quite hostile to the poem's purposes. Thus the theme of the spiritual superiority which results from poverty comes readily to his hand. He can seem to ridicule New Hampshire while actually ennobling it through comparison with the absurd materialism of other regions. There is, then, a serious intent in these comic sketches. Playfully and casually, he develops the image of New Hampshire as a world set apart from ordinary experience, a place where men live by a higher sense of values.

What starts as merely comic implication soon expands to a definition of the New England spirit. One senses that New Hampshire, by its very barrenness, offers a purer way of life and fosters a finer response to experience. This is dramatized by the long final portrait of the repatriated tycoon, a New Hampshire man who has made a fortune selling rags in San Francisco. Because he is "soiled with trade," he is now completely cut off from the life of his native state. Though he lives in New Hampshire, he lives there as an outcast in a fancy mansion

> some ten miles from a railroad station,
> As if to put forever out of mind
> The hope of being, as we say, received.
>
> [ll. 41–3, p. 200]

The poor fellow's fate is not the result of snobbism. We see that through mere money-making he has betrayed the exacting regional standard and is therefore no longer at home where men are expected to live by it.

Having deftly established a contrast between New England and the great outer world, Frost next begins to develop the image of the state as a little world, complete in itself. This is the main purpose of the second part, and the theme of poverty provides a convenient transition:

> Just specimens is all New Hampshire has,
> One each of everything as in a show-case
> Which naturally she doesn't care to sell.
>
> [ll. 61–3, p. 201]

Again and again, we are reminded that New Hampshire produces no *cash* crops. It yields just enough gold to make two sets of engagement and wedding rings, and these, of course, are not sold, but worn by the family on whose land the gold was found. New Hampshire has apples in abundance, but they are only good for cider. And while the state has plenty of farm land, it is so poor that no one (or almost no one) will buy it. Yet, New Hampshire has "One each of everything." It has given the nation one president and one statesman and "the Dartmouth needed to produce him." It has a reformer more impractical than other reformers; it has its enthusiast, a man who raises breeds of chickens mentioned by Chaucer and Herrick; and it has a witch of the old-fashioned kind, not corrupted by modern faddism like the one the poet has met at a "cut-glass dinner" in Boston. It even boasts a legendary prehistoric population. And like the rest of the world, it has its cities which condescend to villages, and villages which condescend to crossroad hamlets.

What Frost is doing here, of course, is to transform New Hampshire into a realm of ideals. He presents it as a rare-fied level of existence where, in place of a confusing plenty, there is an order of representative things, spare and almost insubstantial. The word "specimen" gives us the key to this. We are made to see New Hampshire as a place where everything is somewhat typical. The lack of material wealth serves to reveal the essential nature of things and suggests the interdependence of substance and form. In this world—just because it is poor and remote from the materialism of modern life—objects become the prototypes of ideas.

When Frost turns to discuss the New Hampshire mountains, he at last enters upon his main theme. Part III, which begins here, is concerned with evaluating the region as a subject of poetry. This is indicated by a greater emphasis on the poet's own experiences and opinions. The image of New Hampshire as a world of the imagination has been established, and he now undertakes to explain the role it plays in his own work.

The passage dealing with the New Hampshire mountains should be looked at carefully, for it is through this that Frost sets forth his conception of regional art. As before, his method is that of ironic comment. We are told of certain criticisms raised against New Hampshire. Emerson has said that God "Taunted the lofty land with little men," and Amy Lowell—it is certainly she, though she is not mentioned by name—has advised the poet to reread his own books if he doesn't understand what is wrong with his state.[2] Under the guise of replying to these attacks, Frost

2. That the poetess is Amy Lowell is indicated in this passage:
> Another Massachusetts poet said,
> 'I go no more to summer in New Hampshire.
> I've given up my summer place in Dublin.'
> But when I asked to know what ailed New Hampshire,
> She said she couldn't stand the people in it,
> The little men (it's Massachusetts speaking).

examines the problem of the relation between universals
and particulars. First, he states the issue in terms of his
own writing.

> I may as well confess myself the author
> Of several books against the world in general.
> To take them as against a special state
> Or even nation's to restrict my meaning.
> I'm what is called a sensibilitist,
> Or otherwise an environmentalist.
> I refuse to adapt myself a mite
> To any change from hot to cold, from wet
> To dry, from poor to rich, or back again.
> I make a virtue of my suffering
> From nearly everything that goes on round me.
> In other words, I know wherever I am,
> Being the creature of literature I am,
> I shall not lack for pain to keep me awake.
> Kit Marlowe taught me how to say my prayers:
> 'Why, this is Hell, nor am I out of it.'
> Samoa, Russia, Ireland, I complain of,
> No less than England, France, and Italy.
> Because I wrote my novels in New Hampshire
> Is no proof that I aimed them at New Hampshire.
>
> [ll. 228–47, p. 206]

This passage is the focal point of the poem. It expresses
more clearly than any other lines Frost has written the central fact of his regionalism: that it presents the world of
rural New England, not for its own intrinsic interest, but as

---

And when I asked to know what ailed the people,
She said, 'Go read your own books and find out.'

[ll. 220–7, p. 206]

Miss Lowell summered in Dublin, and in her *Tendencies in Modern
American Poetry* (New York, Macmillan, 1917) she emphasizes the
degeneracy of the New Englanders Frost depicts.

a symbol of the whole world of human experience. "Samoa, Russia, Ireland, I complain of,/ No less than England, France, and Italy." This stands as a reply to Miss Lowell, who insisted that his regional pictures were to be regarded as a "photographic" record of New Hampshire itself. He replies that such a view "restricts my meaning." His books are "against the world in general"; by writing of New England he is really writing of everywhere.

When this is understood, his use of "environmentalist" ceases to seem mere word play. The joke of defining this term in a way quite contrary to Darwin has a serious function: it expresses the paradox at the heart of Frost's regionalism. The more the poet identifies himself with a particular place, the closer he comes to understanding "the world in general." Further, the definition emphasizes the poet's creativity. Whereas in Darwinian evolution the individual is differentiated by his surroundings, Frost's environmentalism describes the opposite process. Instead of being acted upon by his local surroundings, he shapes them to his own purposes: "I make a virtue of my suffering/ From nearly everything that goes on round me." But paradox always has two sides. He is at the same time recognizing the importance of the poet's environment. It is, after all, the medium through which he seeks to portray reality.

Thus he turns next to consider the advantages of this medium. Contradicting Emerson's judgement, he argues that the people of New Hampshire are better than other men. But, he adds, "For art's sake one could almost wish them worse" (l. 266, p. 207): they are too well off and too strong in character to serve as subjects for a true picturing of human suffering. The idea that a sound literature must necessarily portray suffering is one of his most constant assumptions. He is, in many respects, a pessimist and seems to believe that sorrow is an inevitable part of human experience. In the passage we are now considering, however, this idea is a subsidiary theme. We must remember that he is answering Emerson and Amy Lowell. As he wrote these lines, he had particularly in mind her comment that *North of Boston* is a picture of New England decadence. "His people," she wrote, "are left-overs of the old stock, morbid, pursued by phantoms, slowly sinking to insanity." [3] Frost replies that his subject is not the particular griefs and failures of his Yankee characters but the sorrow underlying life itself. His discussion of sorrow in experience and in literature is merely a case in point. Sorrow is universal, and the misery Amy Lowell noted in the people of *North of Boston* serves to show that in writing of regional characters, he writes of all humanity.

The mountains, as I have said, are the dominant image of this section, and when Frost finally comes to describe them they emerge as the culminating symbol of his art. He has been busy contradicting the Emersonian dictum that God "Taunted the lofty land with little men," and having refuted the second part of this pronouncement he now turns to the first. He insists that just as the men are not little, the mountains are not lofty enough. Years ago he saw them depicted as twice their height in a map, and ever since then he has dreamed of what they might be. To the reader who has failed to notice his underlying argument, all this must seem intolerably frivolous. The mountains passage makes sense only when it is recognized as a symbolizing of the poetic process. What seems a mere whim turns out to be an assertion of the poet's creativity:

> If I must choose which I would elevate—
> The people or the already lofty mountains,
> I'd elevate the already lofty mountains.
>
> [ll. 307–9, p. 208]

3. ibid., p. 107.

The reason? Frost does not immediately divulge it. Instead he seems to play with the reader's patience, proposing a number of possible answers only to reject them. In this way a good deal of suspense is developed. After being led to expect much of the final answer we are let down with a feeling of comic anticlimax when the true explanation, so simple and seemingly naive, at last comes out. As we shall see, however, this explanation is not the comically simple answer it appears.

First, however, let us consider the rejected answers (ll. 317–26, p. 209). They are of real interest, for each represents a theory of poetry. The first question ("Can it be some strength/ I feel as of an earthquake in my back") suggests the theory which would explain art in terms of personal talent; the second ("Can it be foreign travel in the Alps?"), the theory that poetry grows from the author's experience; the third ("Or having seen and credited a moment/ The solid molding of vast peaks of cloud/ Behind the pitiful reality/ Of Lincoln, Lafayette, and Liberty?"), the romantic view that poetry springs from moments of mystical vision; the fourth ("Or some such sense as says how high shall jet/ The fountain in proportion to the basin?"), the classical doctrine of natural proportion.

None of these is adequate to explain his regionalism. For him, the poetic process is a reconciling of idea and object, or rather a uniting of the two. It begins when the poet discovers a discrepancy between what he imagines and what he sees. The idea alone is a flat abstraction, like the mountains on the map; but it has a certain fertility, so that once it is discovered, the imagination works unremittingly until it has so changed reality that the idea is embodied in it. While Frost humorously recognizes the humble nature of his inspiration, this only serves to emphasize how great the creative power is which can produce so impressive and meaningful a vision from such material. Thus although his explanation of how he first came to wish the mountains twice their real height at first seems to give us a comic letdown, actually it supplies a more explosive climax than could normally have been expected; just as in the poem as a whole the seeming levity of the poet's manner turns out to be the medium for serious speculation. The poet

> cannot rest from planning day or night
> How high I'd thrust the peaks in summer snow
> To tap the upper sky and draw a flow
> Of frosty night air on the vale below
> Down from the stars to freeze the dew as starry.
>
> [ll. 338–42, p. 209]

The sudden heightening of dignity in these lines has a great dramatic value. One senses that here Frost is touching upon something deeply felt, that we have at last reached the exact center of his thought. This center is the concept of a kind of art in which the regional subject, without ever losing its local identity, is so shaped that it becomes the symbol of an idea. Neither the pure idea, the drawing on the map, nor the reality, the New Hampshire mountains as they actually are, is enough for poetry. The art consists in combining the two. The mountains as the poet imagines them are so exalted that they "tap the upper sky," bringing down a cold celestial air from the stars which in turn forms imitation stars of dew crystals upon earth. The symbolism here is vitally important. In Frost's mind the stars are habitually associated with ideas of astrological influence and an almost Platonic conception of the true, the good, and the beautiful seen as a unity.[4] The regional poet, then, so modifies

4. See especially "The Star-Splitter," "I Will Sing You One-O," and "Choose Something Like a Star."

the local reality as to reach ultimate truth, and in this way he is able to produce in his poems reflections of that truth, the starlike dew crystals. The reader who finds this interpretation difficult is referred to "Evening in a Sugar Orchard," which also deals with the relation between truth and art, and uses a very similar symbolism:

> The sparks made no attempt to be the moon.
> They were content to figure in the trees
> As Leo, Orion, and the Pleiades.
> And that was what the boughs were full of soon.

The reader will perhaps be struck by the similarity between this concept of poetry and the Coleridgean doctrine of the imagination. Indeed, it may appear that what Frost has to tell us about the nature of his own art could be applied to kinds of poetry far different from his. But there is a distinctive element in his theory, the element of regional subject matter. And this makes all the difference. Though the mountains are transformed by the poet's mind into something far more impressive and more meaningful than they are in reality, this transformation is only possible in that he has before him the particular mountains; and these do not lose, but rather augment their particular nature in becoming transformed through art. Poetic theories are always, in one way or another, concerned with the problem of explaining how art reconciles the particular with the universal. In Frost's aesthetic, the particular is identified with the local. He thus solves the problem through a concept of the regional world itself, a world which is at once particular in the extreme and, by virtue of this very particularity, a world of archetypes, or ideas.

This unique conception is summed up in the brilliant climactic scene which brings Part III to a close:

The more the sensibilitist I am
The more I seem to want my mountains wild;
The way the wiry gang-boss liked the log-jam.
After he'd picked the lock and got it started,
He dodged a log that lifted like an arm
Against the sky to break his back for him,
Then came in dancing, skipping, with his life
Across the roar and chaos, and the words
We saw him say along the zigzag journey
Were doubtless as the words we heard him say
On coming nearer: 'Wasn't she an *i*-deal
Son-of-a-bitch? You bet she was an *i*-deal.'

[ll. 343–54, pp. 209–10]

The scene is richly local, and we may take it simply as an exact, almost photographic picture of logging in the New Hampshire backwoods. It illustrates Frost's descriptive skill at its most impressive. The log rising up with a slow, threatening motion is exactly as one would see it. The strange sensation of seeing someone speak without being able to hear him over the deafening roar is caught perfectly. Such imagery has the precision of *trompe-l'oeil*. Yet what emerges from the realistic and thoroughly local scene, what the gang boss has been saying, but is only at last heard when he reaches the shore—is the word *i*-deal! In this word the local and universal are combined. Of course, for the logger the word is just a bit of hyperbolic slang, but its literal meaning embodies the significance of the scene as a whole. The very fact that the logger expresses this meaning inadvertently serves to show the unity of particulars and universals within the regional world. Like the swain of pastoral, he can be lighthearted yet earnest at the same time, because he lives in a sphere where experience is so coherent that fundamental realities emerge from commonplace events.

Frost explicitly compares his own point of view to that of the gang boss. The magnificent confusion of the log jam breaking up, like the poet's dream of mountains raised to the stars, is a vision of the ideal, and we should therefore take the logging scene as an analogy for the poetic process. The gang boss' flight across the stream parallels the poet's maneuvering in the world of ideas. The image points toward Frost's characteristic view of intellectual life as a daring venture into the unknown.

But the poem is still incomplete, for although the logging scene provides a climactic symbol of Frost's theory, this theory has as yet been set forth only in a general way. It is all very well to say that regionalism expresses universals through local particulars, but the reader may well wonder at this point just how this is done. He will need to be convinced of the advantages of such a procedure, to see in some specific case the way in which regional art serves as an imaginative medium for picturing reality. In the poem's final section, therefore, Frost seeks to illustrate his aesthetic.

This section deals with the problem of realism in art. Frost sets it forth in terms of yet another anecdote, this time the account of a conversation he has recently had with "a New York Alec/ About the new school of the pseudo-phallic." This gentleman has attempted to corner the poet. He has argued that a writer must either describe reality without omitting a single aspect, however sordid, or else, by excluding the unpleasant, fall into prudery: " 'Choose you which you will be—a prude, or puke,/ Mewling and puking in the public arms' " (ll. 362-3, p. 210). These, as the New Yorker sees it, are the only alternatives, but the poet balks at both. His reply is characteristic: " 'Me for the hills where I don't have to choose' " (l. 364). The escapism implied in this line must not be misunderstood. As the following lines show, Frost does not mean simply to fly from what is unpleasant in real life. His retreat is the philosophic withdrawal of the pastoralist, who abandons a corrupt world for the purer world of Arcadia in order that he may see reality more clearly. Frost's point here is that in the regional world the conflict between truth and decorum is resolved. This is brilliantly demonstrated in the lines which follow. Here we see the poet restating the problem in terms of pastoral imagery. In this way he not only cleanses the brute facts of sordid associations but, what is much more important, shows that the real issue is not that of sordidness at all. The New York alec has implied that the sordid is an essential part of real life, so that any writer who does not reflect it in his work is merely prudish. And since he is a proponent of the "pseudo-phallic" school, we can assume that he favors a rather realistic treatment of sexual subjects. Frost, though he seems to retreat from this, actually pushes his analysis far beyond it. He sees that sordid things, and particularly the sordid aspects of sex, are merely outward manifestations of nature; the essential problem is not whether the poet should picture sex realistically, but whether he is to take a realistic view of nature itself.

> 'But if you had to choose, which would you be?'
> I wouldn't be a prude afraid of nature.
>
> [ll. 365–6, p. 210]

The real prude, the real escapist, is the person who cannot face the fact that man's physical being connects him with nature. Frost, in an amazingly witty passage, characterizes him as a man afraid to cut down trees and identifies his squeamishness with the humanism of Matthew Arnold:

> he dropped the ax
> And ran for shelter quoting Matthew Arnold:
> 'Nature is cruel, man is sick of blood;
> There's been enough shed without shedding mine.

Remember Birnam Wood! The wood's in flux!'
He had a special terror of the flux
That showed itself in dendrophobia.
The only decent tree had been to mill
And educated into boards, he said.
He knew too well for any earthly use
The line where man leaves off and nature starts,
And never over-stepped it save in dreams.
He stood on the safe side of the line talking;
Which is sheer Matthew Arnoldism . . .[5]

[ll. 369–82, pp. 210–11]

Frost sees that prudery, which for the New Yorker is only
a fear of bad taste in sexual matters, is really something
much more basic: a fear of man's natural condition, of the
"flux," of organic vitality. Hence the contrast between the
dead boards and the living trees.

On the other hand, the puke—the writer whose art is
entirely realistic—is also shown to be at fault. Here again,
Frost's method of restating the problem in regional terms
enables him to clarify it. The real mistake of the puke is
not that he offends good taste through obscenity—his obscenity is just a consequence of his unreasonable view of
nature; his effort to reflect reality exactly results from his
placing too high a value upon physical truths. In the end,
he prefers the material to the human, and raises altars of
superstition in the woods:

Even to say the groves were God's first temples
Comes too near to Ahaz' sin for safety.
Nothing not built with hands of course is sacred.

[ll. 392–4, p. 211]

5. In the lines immediately following this passage, there is a curious
confusion on Frost's part. He seems to apply to Arnold the phrase, "took
dejectedly/ His seat upon the intellectual throne," whereas in "The
Scholar-Gypsy," stanza 19, from which these words are taken, Arnold
applies them to another poet, presumably Tennyson.

He is the tree-worshipper, whose naturalism is identified with the idolatry of Ahaz and the shameful rites of the grove.

The last section, then, is to be understood as a dramatizing of pastoralist's method itself. We are shown how the poet resolves a problem which in the context of sophisticated urban life seems insurmountable by projecting it into the simple, idealized world of rural New Hampshire. In this way he is able not only to escape the dilemma posed by the New Yorker, but to see the problem much more clearly than his antagonist. He strips away the outer husks which conceal reality, discovering beneath the narrow question of realism in art the broader and more fundamental issue of man's whole relation to nature. Thus "Me for the hills," far from being an anguished call to retreat, is the option for a more penetrating exploration of reality. Of course, there is implicit in it too the idea of withdrawal. At the end Frost is more than a little complacent at the thought that in New Hampshire the poet's mind is freed from the distractions of a more complicated world. It is, as he says, "a most restful state." But one should remember that he is playing upon a major theme of pastoral, present in the classical eclogues and reinforced in the Renaissance by the authority of Christian asceticism: the idea that retreat to the rural world purifies the mind and thus brings it closer to ultimate truth. And indeed, the very form of the poem embodies this theme. The poet casts himself as the folksy rural sage, just as the courtier in the old pastoral took on the guise of the shepherd. His casual speaking manner, which digresses at every turning into anecdote and whimsical speculation, creates the illusion that the poem is just a specimen of back-parlor conversation. But as it turns out, his random comments prove to be the medium for dealing with matters which are very serious indeed, so that there is more than a little irony in the contrast between the speaker's apparent and actual intent.

"New Hampshire" is not a perfect poem, and I would hesitate to claim it as one of Frost's best. It is a satire, so that the reader who finds he cannot like it would do well to consider whether his attitude toward the genre is not the cause. In any case, the poem is of great value to the reader who has a serious interest in Frost's poetry, for here the basic function of his regionalism is defined and the ideas tacitly assumed in his other New England poems are made explicit. That Frost himself clearly recognized its special status is shown by the way in which he first presented it to the public. He published it in his fourth book, *New Hampshire: A Poem with Notes and Grace Notes,* where it stands as the central, unifying work, the other pieces being linked to it as if they were merely more detailed commentary. The longer of these other poems, "The Star-Splitter" and "The Witch of Coös," for example, are the "notes," and the lyrics the "grace notes." It has been said that this arrangement was just a harmless joke, reflecting upon Eliot's use of notes in *The Waste Land.* This may be true, but Frostian jokes seldom lack a serious purpose, and though the arrangement may have been an afterthought it is nevertheless significant. It indicates that "New Hampshire" defines the point of view from which the other regional poems are written. As the poet himself reports, it was late on the night when he finished this poem that he wrote "Stopping by Woods," one of his finest pastoral lyrics.

The great value of "New Hampshire" is that it illustrates the pastoral design of Frost's poetry. It shows us that his rural New England is a world of symbol, and that his method as a regional poet is that of exploring the other worlds of experience through this world. New England represents the poet's mode of thought, but we must not take it as an entirely subjective vision. It is a place as well as a post of observation, and, indeed, its value for the poet depends upon its objective reality. In his poems the reader's attention is focused directly upon the things depicted: the characters and rural scenes seem to exist in their own right, and their symbolic import is a function of their reality. Ultimately, it is Frost's devotion to regional New England that enables him to reveal within the particular local facts realities which extend to far distant ranges of experience.

CHAPTER 3

THE YANKEE MANNER: STYLE AS SYMBOL

The Yankee manner, for which Frost has been so often and so deservedly praised, is something more than a mere technical achievement. Every poet, of course, must find or create his idiom, and Frost's, when he finally achieves it in the poems of *North of Boston,* is an amazingly subtle mode of expression. Everyone must be impressed by his nice sense of language and delicacy in handling tonal effects. But expressiveness is not its only value. What is more important is Frost's ability to make the language itself function as an image. His Yankee manner is not only a way of speaking; it is the symbol of a mode of thought. By representing the thought process of his Yankee speaker, it becomes a means of picturing the regional world itself.

While Frost's critics have been unanimous in commending his style, they have not gone very far toward explaining it. Some have claimed that the poet does no more than copy regional speech, as if to say that his handling of language is simply a very accurate kind of phonetic notation. Others tend toward the all too attractive theory of mystical kinship. For example, Cornelius Weygandt writes:

> Wordsworth fits no more perfectly into the background of England's Lake Country than Frost into the background of New Hampshire. Hot-heartedly indi-

vidual as Frost is, with an intensity of lyric feeling,
and a keenness of vision, and a firmness of artistry independent of place and time, there is much of New
Hampshire in him . . . All rural New England
shares a laconic speech, a picturesqueness of phrase,
a stiffness of lip, a quizzicality of attitude, a twistiness
of approach to thought, but there is a New Hampshire
slant to all these qualities, and that slant you find in
the verse of Frost.[1]

In other words, Frost gives us regional speech just as it is,
because he knows it, he hears it and, above all, he *shares* it.

Most critics, however, prefer to explain Frost's style as
a matter of pure technique. They speak of craftsmanship
and imply that the poet has discovered some trick way of
contriving tonal and metrical effects. There is much talk of
his ability to choose the right words and to catch the precise rhythm of a voice, but the secret of just *how* this is
done is never divulged. One suspects it never will be, for
this view assumes that his style is to be explained in terms
of verbal mechanics alone. This is implicit, for example,
in Robert S. Newdick's remark that "Frost has addressed
himself for forty-odd years primarily to the fundamental
problems involved in capturing in poetry the full range of
tones in the speech of living men and women." [2] And Mark
Van Doren writes in the same vein: "His strangeness (here
a term of praise) consisted, and still consists, in the conversational tone he builds into his verse." [3] Frost himself has
done much to encourage such an approach. The following
excerpt from a conversation shows his characteristic emphasis upon technique:

1. "New Hampshire," in *Recognition of Robert Frost,* ed. Richard
Thornton, p. 65.
2. "Robert Frost and the Sound of Sense," *American Literature, 9*
(1937), 289.
3. "The Permanence of Robert Frost," in *Recognition,* p. 6.

The visual images thrown up by a poem are important, but it is more important still to choose and arrange words in a sequence so as virtually to control the intonations and pauses of the reader's voice. By the arrangement and choice of words on the part of the poet, the effects of humor, pathos, hysteria, anger, and, in fact, all effects, can be indicated and obtained.[4]

And on another occasion he put the matter even more forcefully:

Let us take the example of two people who are talking to each other on the other side of a closed door, whose voices can be heard but whose words cannot be distinguished. Even though the words do not carry, the sound of them does, and the listener can catch the meaning of the conversation. This is because every meaning has a particular sound-posture, or, to put it another way, the sense of every meaning has a particular sound which each individual is instinctively familiar with . . .[5]

Frost's purpose, of course, was to emphasize the importance of sound and rhythm. He wished to remind us that in speech the movement of a sentence is an expression of its sense, the accents, the pauses, the voice's rise and fall evoking a feeling which exactly fits the tenor of what is said. To this one can readily assent; but Frost goes even further. He seems to imply that the sound, taken by itself, conveys meaning. The listener at the door can get the meaning of the conversation within even though he cannot make out

4. Newdick, p. 298. This statement originally appeared in "A Poet on the Campus of the University of Michigan," *Detroit News* (Nov. 27, 1921), Part 7, p. 1.

5. ibid., p. 292. This statement originally appeared in "Robert Frost, New American Poet," *Boston Evening Transcript* (May 8, 1915), Part 3, pp. 4, 10.

the words. This, to my mind, seems very doubtful. Of course the listener would be able to tell whether the speakers were arguing or just having a friendly chat, but it is unlikely that he could tell exactly what they were saying. Frost may have overstated the case for the sake of emphasis, and it would not be fair to take remarks made casually in conversation as a final statement of his view. Nevertheless his tendency to stress the mechanical aspects of arranging sounds and pauses does create the impression that his style is purely a matter of sound patterning. Perhaps from the poet's point of view it is natural to think of style in this way, for in his writing he has to give close attention to technical problems. But sound and rhythm constitute only one aspect of style, and this cannot be properly understood unless it is seen in relation to the others.

"The Grindstone" provides a good illustration of Frost's Yankee manner, and by examining his prosody as we find it here we will be able to see just how far the mechanical analysis of style will carry us. Let us consider the first paragraph:

I	Having a wheel and four legs of its own
I	Has never availed the cumbersome grindstone
R	To get it anywhere that I can see.
R	These hands have helped it go, and even race;
r	Not all the motion, though, they ever lent,
r	Not all the miles it may have thought it went,
r	Have got it one step from the starting place.
r	It stands beside the same old apple tree.
r	The shadow of the apple tree is thin
R	Upon it now, its feet are fast in snow.
	All other farm machinery's gone in,
r	And some of it on no more legs and wheel
	Than the grindstone can boast to stand or go.
I	(I'm thinking chiefly of the wheelbarrow.)

R   For months it hasn't known the taste of steel,
     Washed down with rusty water in a tin.
     But standing outdoors hungry, in the cold,
R   Except in towns at night, is not a sin.
r   And, anyway, its standing in the yard
I   Under a ruinous live apple tree
R   Has nothing any more to do with me,
R   Except that I remember how of old
r   One summer day, all day I drove it hard,
r   And someone mounted on it rode it hard,
R   And he and I between us ground a blade. [1–25]

The meter is iambic pentameter, and at least eight of the twenty-five lines are perfectly regular. On the other hand, several lines show striking departures; for example, the second, "Hăs névĕr ăváiled thĕ cúmbĕrsŏme gríndstóne," and the twentieth, "Úndĕr ă rúinŏus líve ápple trée." There are about four lines of this sort. The remainder fall somewhere in between, but one should note that most of them are only slightly irregular, having just one foot which is not iambic. These are indicated at the left of the lines by a small *r*, the perfect lines by a large *R*, and the very irregular lines (those having at least three variants) by a large *I*. The four unmarked lines are ones which have either one or two variants, depending on the reader's preference. Admittedly, this kind of analysis does not do justice to the subtle variations in degree of stress or pause. Should "grindstone" in line two be accounted a trochee or a spondee? The second syllable calls for less stress than the first, but whether the second stress is strong enough for a spondee is debatable. Scanning is always rather crude and arbitrary, and I therefore do not claim to be precise in my judgments on the meter of this passage; but though the reader may disagree with details, he will have to conclude that on the whole the rhythm is quite regular. I have tried to scan every doubtful foot as irregular rather than regular, but a glance at the symbols beside the lines will show that even when the passage is read in this way, the regular lines and those showing only minor variants far outnumber the others. Furthermore, there is a consistent tendency to anapaestic rhythms, and almost all the variants result from substitution of an anapaest for an iamb, so that even the irregularities are almost regular.

These technicalities are worth noting because they show that in terms of rhythm alone Frost's practice does not involve any very unusual innovations. Almost all of his poems are written in traditional meters. The movement is usually iambic and, with rare exceptions, the lines are of four or five feet. His procedure is to establish a strong rhythmic pattern and then play against it a number of more or less wide variations. It hardly needs pointing out that this has been the normal practice in English poetry since the Renaissance. Perfect regularity is neither possible nor desirable. The emphasis which the meaning of the words demands always pulls more or less against the regular cadence, and the actual rhythm of a poem is the net result of this tension. But poets differ in the kind and number of their variations. Comparing Frost with the major poets before 1900, I think it is safe to say that he uses wider and more frequent variations. He is not really any more conservative than certain other moderns—Yeats and Auden, for instance; yet at the same time he is certainly not an innovator. While such poets as Pound and Cummings have developed new kinds of rhythms, Frost has only adapted the old meters, and such changes as he has made are moderate.

Nevertheless, there is something distinctive in his handling of rhythm. One sees it here in his ability to maintain a strong, regular cadence and yet make the lines seem loose and unpatterned. The looseness can be traced to the many spondees and clusters of unaccented syllables, which break up the meter again and again without ever displacing it. It is not displaced because the variations, though numerous, are balanced by the frequent reiteration of the meter in perfect lines. Syllable count as well is strictly observed: only one of the twenty-five lines in this passage has more than ten syllables, none less. The result is a rhythm which has the advantages of regular meter, and yet creates an abrupt and rough effect suggestive of everyday speech.

But rhythm alone is not enough to create the speaking tone—one cannot imitate the sound of conversation simply by writing in irregular lines. Furthermore, the passage is not only speech, but regional speech, yet it would be absurd to claim that the Yankee accent is reducible to any formula of stresses and pauses.

A saner view would be that Frost's rhythms seem regional because the casual quality we have noticed is combined with distinctly local diction, but this too is wide of the mark. In the seventy-seven lines of "The Grindstone" there is not a single dialect word or phrase, and, though I have searched conscientiously, I can find only five or six localisms in the whole of his work.[6] Frost is not a dialect poet either in the sense that he uses regional words or spells other words so as to indicate a local pronunciation. He seems to have recognized from the first that dialect forms attract too much attention to themselves and have a tendency to produce ludicrous effects. Furthermore, the attempt to write poetry in dialect is almost always self-defeating. Lowell's meticulous recording of Yankee pro-

6. A few examples of what looks like dialect pronunciation are: "*i*-deal" in "New Hampshire," ll. 353-4, p. 210; "ile" for "oil" in "Brown's Descent," last stanza; the rhyming of "Ira" with "inquiry" in "Of the Stones of the Place." Even in such rare cases the pronunciation need not always be regarded as peculiar to New England. For example, "*i*-deal" appears in other localities.

nunciation in *The Biglow Papers* sounds much less like speech than Frost's plain English.

It is colloquial usage rather than dialect that distinguishes his style. Every English-speaking person may be said to know two tongues—the formal, more tightly organized literary language and the language of everyday speech. Frost consistently writes in the manner of the spoken rather than the written word. But in adapting the colloquial language to poetry, he purifies it. Everyday speech tends to be slangy and allows for careless inaccuracies in the use of many words. Frost recognizes that the essence of colloquial English is its phrasing rather than its diction, and in his verse it is this that he imitates. Take the opening sentence of "The Grindstone":

> Having a wheel and four legs of its own
> Has never availed the cumbersome grindstone
> *To get it anywhere that I can see.*

The last line is certainly unlike literary usage, yet none of the words are outside the pale of written English. The colloquial quality is in the idioms and the casual way one follows the other. The same may be said for phrases like "farm machinery's gone in" and "Has nothing any more to do with me."

Frost's constant preference for the phrasing of everyday speech is related to the looseness we have found in his rhythms. Colloquialisms have a certain wordiness. They tend to be roundabout and vague in syntactical connection, since in conversation the speaker cannot attend too closely to matters of syntax. He therefore avoids an obviously tight sentence structure. He contrives to make his sentences seem to ramble, weaving in loosely related modifiers and interrupting with asides. There are few abrupt stops or sharp transitions from point to point. The speaker seems to wander carelessly from one thing to another, and it is

only when we look back across a paragraph that we see
how compactly the poet has fitted together his materials.
Consider, for example, the last sentence of our passage. The
clauses are joined in the loosest possible way:

> *And, anyway,* its standing in the yard
> Under a ruinous live apple tree
> Has nothing any more to do with me,
> *Except that* I remember how of old
> One summer day, all day I drove it hard,
> *And* someone mounted on it rode it hard,
> *And* he and I between us ground a blade.

It is this very weakness of the connectives that allows Frost
to give the reader important bits of information in the
briefest and most direct way. If each thought were put in
an independent sentence which showed clearly its logical
relation to the other thoughts, the passage would be several
lines longer, and it would seem too neat to sound like common speech. The loose syntax and the wordiness go together; they belong to the same level of language, and they
reflect the same informality we have seen in the poet's variations of meter.

If Frost's style were no more than an imitation of everyday speech, our investigation could stop here, for it would
seem that his technique is simply that of combining a
somewhat irregular meter with colloquial idiom. But the
reader will suspect that there is much more to it. How are
we to account for the peculiarly regional quality of his
lines? And how does the poet create the impression that a
living person speaks these lines? We must remember that
Frost is working in the printed, not the spoken word. He
cannot reproduce the intonation of Yankee speech but
must imitate it, and no particular rhythm will accomplish
this. I am sure that the rhythm of any line in Frost could
be paralleled in lines in the work of other poets where the

tone is entirely different. Nor can we find the answer in
Frost's use of colloquialisms, for as the work of dozens of
minor local colorists shows us, a poet may fill his lines with
the phrases of everyday conversation and still fail to capture the speaking tone. The fact is that no rhythmic pattern, no technique of phrasing, no system of poetic diction
taken by itself can explain the dramatic and regional qualities of Frost's style; and even when all these are taken together they do not account for it. This is so because in his
verse, as in all good poetry, the way a thing is written is a
part of its meaning. As soon as one isolates stylistic elements, they lose their meaning and thus their essential
nature. The amount of stress the words in a poem get is
largely determined by what the line says, and that, in turn,
by what the poem as a whole says. Similarly, the sound tone
of a phrase grows out of its emotional tone, which depends
on the attitudes implicit in other parts of the poem. The
style, then, is not distinct from the content of poetry;
rather it is that part of a poem where we see the meaning
reflected in and *symbolized by* the details of language. The
only way we will ever get at the essential nature of Frost's
style is by seeing the stylistic elements in their organic
relation to the meaning of his poems.

The link between style and meaning is the character of
the person who speaks Frost's lines. What Frost has said of
poetry in general applies with especial force to his own
work:

> A dramatic necessity goes deep into the nature of
> the sentence. Sentences are not different enough to
> hold the attention unless they are dramatic. No inge-
> nuity of varying structure will do. All that can save
> them is the speaking tone of voice somehow entangled
> in the words and fastened to the page for the ear of the
> imagination.[7]

7. Preface to *A Way Out* (New York, Harbor Press, 1929), pp. [iii-iv].

His ability to catch the inflections of Yankee speech springs from this sense of the dramatic. In his poems one hears the speaking voice and knows that the language is genuine, because the speaker is dramatically conceived. Frost came closest to explaining his actual method of composition when he said that he begins a poem by imagining "the tone of someone speaking and as the form of a simple meter." [8] The speaker and the speech rhythm are not invented separately; the meter is that of someone speaking. The whole manner of speaking is embodied in that *someone*.

Now it is Frost's way of imagining the speaker that concerns us. He conceives him, I think, as a many-sided and complex character, one who has a certain standard of values and a particular way of thought. Most often, this speaker is a rural New Englander. His attitudes, his moral sense and, indeed, his whole mentality dramatize the regional world and therefore function as symbols to represent it. His personality is revealed through his manner of speaking, and since it is he who utters the poem, his manner of speaking is the poem's style. In his character we can see the union of style and content. Here the Yankee manner can be recognized as a vital part, not only of the poem's meaning, but of its pastoral structure. For it is to a large extent through style that Frost represents the Yankee point of view and thus establishes the contrast between the rural world and common experience. But the process is reciprocal. Just as the Yankee manner defines the regional theme, the theme in turn infuses the style with a distinctly local flavor.

To see just how this is done, let us turn back again to "The Grindstone." The poem is a fine example of Frost's pastoralism. Here, as in so many of his other rural pieces, a trivial incident is developed into a symbol of serious issues.

8. Reginald L. Cook, "Robert Frost's Asides on His Poetry," *American Literature, 19* (1948), 355.

The speaker casually describes the old grindstone in the yard and then goes on to relate how he once worked at the wheel all one afternoon to grind a blade. Gradually, as the bits of descriptive detail begin to accumulate, one realizes that the grindstone is an analogue for the world. It stands under the shadow of "a ruinous live apple tree," its shape worn down through centuries of use to "an oblate / Spheroid." [9] It turns on its axis, and it tilts and wobbles in turning as the world does in relation to the sun from season to season. It is inconceivably old and may once have ground arrowheads as it now grinds metal blades. Its violent motion can almost result in "disaster." It is hard, indifferent, proud, and seems to hate the men who work on it. And finally, its song is the "gritty tune" of discord.

The analogy extends to the two grinders. They represent two aspects of human creativity. The speaker, whose job it is to make the wheel go round, symbolizes the effort and suffering of man's work. The "Father-Time-like man" who works with him represents the other essential aspect of creativity. It is his job to hold the blade to the stone. In doing so he resists the speaker's efforts to turn the wheel,

9. For the idea of the analogy between the grindstone and the world I am indebted to Mr. Norman Holmes Pearson, who has made available to me a letter from Frost in which the poet comments on "The Grindstone" as follows: "If you had permitted me one nomination it might have been 'The Grindstone,' a favorite of mine and to me 'an image of the naughty world.' You know Herschel had a grindstone theory of the universe." Mr. Pearson reports that actually this comparison did not originate with Herschel. It seems to have been suggested first by Simon Newcomb in discussing Herschel's theory of the shape of the universe. The relevant passage from Newcomb is as follows:

> A century ago Sir William Herschel reached the conclusion that our universe was composed of a comparatively thin but widely extended stratum of stars. To introduce a familiar object, its figure was that of a large, thin grindstone, our solar system being near the center. Considering only the general aspect of the heavens, this conclusion was plausible. [*The Stars: A Study of the Universe* (New York, Putnam, 1908), p. 233.]

yet only through this counterpressure can the blade be ground. His role in the work points toward his symbolic meaning. Two aspects of him are important: his cold indifference to the speaker and his role as the final judge. It is he who controls the work, and it is he who in his own good time will decide when the blade is perfectly sharpened. He will not be satisfied with one hairbreadth less than perfection, no matter how long and hard the speaker has to work. The speaker sweats; he "rides." Between the two workers there is a natural animosity. They are working together, but they must do so by working *against* each other.

Their relation is the vital point. The old man holding the blade is compared to Father Time with his scythe, so that to some extent he is an image of mortality and hence the speaker's opponent. The speaker does no more than turn the wheel; the intelligence, without which nothing could be created, is that of the old man. The two men may be said to embody the Dionysian and the Apollonian principles, the one natural energy, the other pure intellect. But since the grindstone symbolizes the world, I am tempted to see them also as to some extent suggesting the flesh and the devil. The grindstone is hard and purposeless. The speaker errs in wanting to give up too soon because he suffers physically, while the old man tends to sin through pride in that he aims at perfection. He would make the blade exactly "all it should be" and will not leave the final touch to "the whetter." But the poem is too complex for schematic explanations, and I make this suggestion only as a way of showing how deeply Frost's symbolism penetrates to the moral issues involved in man's work.

Creativity means suffering and sacrifice; it also requires an inflexible standard, something human in that it is conceived by man's mind but inhuman in that it is a coldly abstract ideal and cannot, by the nature of things, be altered

to spare the individual. Hence the old man lacks all com-
passion for the speaker and is concerned only with the
thought of just how sharp the blade should be ground.
Man cannot create except in terms of such an ideal, and
thus the ideal is part of human nature; but man's effort to
realize the ideal (even in the very humble task of grinding
a blade) is a usurping of divinity. Therefore man's ability
to create inevitably involves him in evil:

> I could have cried
> Wasn't there danger of a turn too much?
> Mightn't we make it worse instead of better?
> I was for leaving something to the whetter.
> What if it wasn't all it should be? I'd
> Be satisfied if he'd be satisfied.

After all, it is the use that counts, and the final touch
should be left to the whetter. The attempt to make all perfect beforehand is a way of playing God.

The complex and important ethical issue at the center
of this little scene is brilliantly symbolized by "the blade"
which the two men are making. Since the setting is a farmyard, it would be natural for them to be sharpening some
farm implement—a sickle, for instance—but Frost never
lets us know what it is. Instead, he consistently calls it a
blade. On the realistic level, it must be a tool of some sort,
but the more general term "blade" suggests the soldier's
sword or the criminal's dagger as well as the farmer's sickle.
Thus the blade figures forth the ambiguous nature of
man's creativity: what he creates could be an instrument
of either good or evil, just as the act of creating itself involves both virtue and error. The great strength of the
symbolism is that it recognizes the human dilemma as necessary and inescapable. To produce a thing of value, man
must sacrifice his own natural desires, submit to suffering,

and impose a cruelly tyrannical standard upon himself. Most important, he must strive to go beyond his own ability, which means a denial of self and a dangerous kind of presumption.

That this little episode expresses anything as profound as the interdependence of good and evil may seem surprising, since the way it is presented appears to be casual, even amusing. But in pastoral the serious and the humorous, the important and the humble commonplace are not opposites—it has always been a genre which treats important matters in an unpretentious manner. This is another way of asserting the pastoral poet's indirection, a quality which one sees here in the way Frost abstains from open explanations. The two men working at the grindstone have an allegorical meaning, but this is nowhere stated in explicit terms. Rather, the deeper meaning is suggested by the way in which they are described. Thus, when we come to consider just how Frost indicates his symbolic intent we are brought back to the vital function of style. The style of the poem is the speaking manner of the Yankee *persona* who utters the lines. The way he speaks reveals his character, his standards of judgment, his mode of thinking, and it is therefore the style that makes us aware of the hidden significance he sees beneath the surface of his experience. By symbolizing his attitudes, the style interprets what he tells us.

As we have seen, the speaker approaches his subject in a beguilingly casual way. He begins with what seems like a merely playful description of the grindstone, and it is only when we are well into the poem that we come to recognize his symbolic intent. Even his most direct intimations are jocular in tone—for example, "I gave it the preliminary spin,/ And poured on water (tears it might have been)." Throughout he keeps up a pretense of scornful indifference, so that one is led to feel that the whole poem

is no more than the recollection of an annoying experience. He describes what is after all only an unpleasant hour
or two of work, and his antagonists—though he admits that
they *are* antagonists—are just a grindstone and a ridiculous
old man.

But this casualness on the part of the speaker is really
the means of implying more serious things. The more he
makes light of his work at the grindstone, the more we
become aware that his manner is one of ironic understatement. He is not indifferent. His flippant remarks all
serve to show a rigorous self-discipline in his character:

> Not for myself was I so much concerned.
> Oh no!—although, of course, I could have found
> A better way to pass the afternoon.

This restraint implies a remarkable tough-mindedness.
We sense that he is too acutely aware of the complexity
in what he is describing to sacrifice any aspect of the truth
by reducing it to easy generalizations. His manner symbolizes a way of thinking which is sure, subtle, penetrating. Furthermore, it leads us still deeper into the speaker's
character in that it implies a very high ethical standard:
the speaker puts so great an evaluation upon truth that he
will not falsify what he sees by simple explanations. In
other words, his indirection is a way of expressing the most
complicated meanings and thus makes us aware that the
little episode of the grindstone, though it may seem unimportant, has a very wide significance.

But this special intelligence is not enough to make the
speaker a living person. To seem really human he must feel
as well as think, and Frost is as much concerned to show
his feelings about the experience he describes as to reveal
his understanding of it. The poem not only explores the
nature of man's work, but through the speaker it dramatizes the complex of human feelings toward the experience

of working. We see this in the nice balance between the speaker's good humor and his rather rueful misgivings. There is in him a willingness to submit to the old man, but mixed with this an annoyance, a sense of the futility of endless, unrewarding effort and an uneasy doubt that perhaps the standard is too exacting, that too much is required of mortal flesh. We get both resignation and protest, both laughter and chagrin, a strange blending which pervades the whole poem. For example, the old man tries out the blade:

> he raised it dripping once and tried
> The creepy edge of it with wary touch,
> And viewed it over his glasses funny-eyed.

In the speaker's tone the clash between amusement and scorn creates the complex effect of real emotion.

We see, then, that the speaking tone and Yankee quality result from Frost's ability to conceive his speaker as a complex dramatic character. The very form of the poem illustrates this. The poem is presented as a specimen of conversation, and the casual way in which first one and then another bit of information is brought in portrays the indirection and subtlety of the speaker's line of thought. And when we turn from the general structure to the more technical aspects of style, we find that here too the illusion of speech is caused by the technique of making the style point toward the speaker's mentality. Let us look again at the opening sentence:

> Having a wheel and four legs of its own
> Has never availed the cumbersome grindstone
> To get it anywhere that I can see.

Obviously the phrasing of the third line is colloquial, yet the mere presence of such idiom is not enough to make the sentence sound like speech. Frost has caught the sound of speech because he has been able to use the colloquial idiom to suggest a particular attitude. "To get somewhere" connotes a kind of movement that is less efficient and purposeful than "to go" or "to travel." It implies clumsiness, great efforts for small results; and the grindstone, despite its wheel and four legs, has not even been able to move in this way. The idiom voices scorn and skepticism as to the grindstone's value. But this is not all. The phrase also implies that the grindstone ought to get itself somewhere, and since grindstones aren't made for physical travel, it becomes clear that the movement the speaker has in mind is purely figurative—improvement, progress, or something of the sort. Frost is using the colloquial idiom for its full implications. He has not brought it in merely to give his lines the right conversational tone. The idiom helps to show that the speaker views the grindstone, and indeed the whole episode he recounts, symbolically.

The vagueness and casual quality of the colloquialisms enables Frost to hint at the underlying significance in just the right way. He does not wish to make his symbolism flatly mechanical, because the meaning will only be convincing if it grows naturally out of the realistic details of the scene. The reader must see it as if he were actually on the scene himself; in other words, the very process of perception must be dramatized. Hence the importance of the speaker. He tells us of his own experience, and in experience one does not read the meanings of things like neatly written labels, but rather the significance glows dimly beneath the surface. Frost is able to portray the speaker in the very act of seeing, because he presents the poem as a tentative exploration, an awareness of the hidden depths and dark areas of uncertainty. Ironically, the qualities which make colloquial idiom seem unsuited for serious literature are for Frost the very means of showing the speaker's superior perceptiveness. The vagueness of the idiom serves as a way of subtly indicating the complications of what he sees. The casual attitude it suggests expresses the careful restraint of one who will not let his feelings confuse him in his cautious searching of reality.

I have discussed only one phrase, but the same symbolic process may be found in numerous other colloquialisms. For example:

> I wondered what machine of ages gone
> This represented *an improvement on.*
> *For all I knew* it may have sharpened spears
> And arrowheads itself.

Everywhere Frost's colloquialisms are used not only to reveal the speaker's mind, but to portray the Yankee traits of that mind. This is why in his verse the everyday language spoken throughout America appears to be a unique Yankee speech.

Nor is this technique used only in the longer poems where the New England setting is obvious. In his lyrics Frost manages his style in much the same way. Here, of course, the canvas is smaller, with the result that the poet has far less space to elaborate the regional traits of his speaker. Even so, he consistently views things through the eyes of the New England *persona,* and as a matter of fact, the greater compression of the lyric makes the method more apparent. Only a few deft touches in the style are needed to portray the regional speaker.

"Fire and Ice," for example, is not an overtly regional poem, yet its power results mainly from the regional values implicit in the speaker's tone. On first reading, one is most impressed by the bold metaphors, and the poem's value would appear to consist in the care with which Frost has developed them. Yet actually, Frost's success here depends upon his perfect control of style. What makes the poem interesting is not only the content of its statements but the

point of view from which they are uttered. The more one
listens to the nuances of tone, the more one hears the
Yankee qualities of the speaker's voice:

> Some say the world will end in fire,
> Some say in ice.
> From what I've tasted of desire
> I hold with those who favor fire.
> But if it had to perish twice,
> I think I know enough of hate
> To say that for destruction ice
> Is also great
> And would suffice.

The real life of the poem is the speaker's awareness.
While he does not talk about any event of his own life,
his words vibrate with the consciousness of experience
acutely felt. How does Frost achieve this effect? The emotion is one of such intense bitterness that one may assume
the poet works through exaggeration. This is true so far as
the imagery is concerned. By the linking of desire to fire
and hate to ice, human emotions are transformed into vast,
impersonal forces. In terms of imagery alone the poem is
extremely rich, and one could find great complexity of
meaning in the paradoxes it reveals, as, for example, in
the idea that the intensity of man's passions, the very
thing which makes him human, creates the inhuman forces
of cataclysm.

But the metaphors would be much less powerful were
it not for the harsh, tight-lipped manner in which the lines
are spoken. What gives the poem its intensity is something
just the opposite of exaggeration, the speaker's persistent
understatement. Throughout the poem the homey, informal, dryly factual manner of speaking plays against the
strong emotion and seriousness of what is said. As a record
of colloquial English the poem is a tour de force. Consider

the daring of Frost's language: the speaker is at one moment casual ("Some say"), at the next politely reticent ("From what I've tasted of desire"), then homespun ("I hold with those who favor fire"), then jocular ("But if it had to perish twice"), then modest, self-effacing ("I think I know enough of hate"), and at last coolly practical ("for destruction ice / Is also great / And would suffice"). The colloquial phrasing does not negate the poem's bitterness. Quite the opposite; it is the means of raising it to an extreme pitch. The more the speaker's manner disclaims strong feelings, the more powerful his feelings seem. Furthermore, the understatement dramatizes the special character of the Yankee swain. His ironic, casual manner manifests a more than normal sensitivity of thought. He is speaking of things in human nature which arouse the deepest terror, but he will not yield to emotional outbursts. Instead he holds back, pretending to be amused, indifferent, because only by reining in his own feelings can he be free to face the brutal results of man's emotions realistically or recognize their full destructiveness.

I have said that the poem is bitter, but this does not mean that its meaning is pessimistic. The holocaust of desire and glaciers of hate are balanced by the honesty and courage of the speaker who is able to see them for what they are. Furthermore, we see in his character that man is capable of judging by an exalted standard of goodness, for only in terms of such a standard could he feel such horror in contemplating the human passions. Here again, Frost's use of colloquial idiom illustrates the pastoral structure of his style. It is the humble, everyday phrase that serves as a medium for expressing the most serious ideas, just as elsewhere it is the simple, rural scene that represents the world as a whole.

Frost's achievement as a stylist is due to his ability to transform the style itself into a symbol. As I have said, his

Yankee manner is not only a medium for expressing regional attitudes, it is also an image of them. We have seen how he uses language to dramatize the thought of his speaker and thus to make him a distinct personality. The speaker, however, in addition to being an individual, is also the regional spokesman, and the style defines a way of thought typical of the whole rural society. A point made in the preceding chapter bears repeating here: Frost always stops short of being a completely personal poet, for his individualism is balanced by, and, indeed, justified by a system of values which lies beyond the individual. To penetrate to this area of shared beliefs is no easy task, especially since there reticence itself is one of the more important principles. We are not dealing with conscious precepts, but with a complex of tacit assumptions. And Frost, like Eliot and Hemingway, who maintain a similar reserve, avoids spelling out these beliefs, for he wishes to show them as they exist in the mind.

The symbolic function of style is best illustrated in "The Code," where the Yankee manner is the subject as well as the medium. The title deserves attention, for it points directly to the poem's theme. The word "code" has two meanings. It can signify either a system of communication or an ethical standard. In this poem Frost uses both meanings simultaneously, for his subject is the unity of the two. He wishes to show that the rural New Englander's special way of communicating and his ultimate beliefs are inseparable, that both are aspects of the same thought process. Thus "the code" is a symbol of the coherence of regional life. It joins the individual to the community through a bond of shared customs and beliefs, and what is more important, it combines thought and belief. In the Yankee code, one is a function of the other. The way of communicating is a value, and, conversely, Yankee values are the cause of this elaborate system of signals.

Before beginning the main narrative, the poet dramatizes the code by means of a brief frame story. The scene
is a meadow at haying time, where three men are working
desperately to cock the hay before an approaching storm.
One is a city-bred farmer, the other two, his Yankee hired
hands. All of a sudden one of the Yankees throws down
his pitchfork angrily and leaves for home. The farmer cannot understand why he has quit, and so the remaining
hired man, realizing that his boss is ignorant of Yankee
ways, offers to explain. A half hour before, the farmer had
said something about their taking pains. He had meant
nothing by this; he was only thinking out loud, but the
Yankee took his remark as an implied reproach.

> He thought you meant to find fault with his work.
> That's what the average farmer would have meant.
> James would take time, of course, to chew it over
> Before he acted: he'd just got round to act.

This misunderstanding establishes the pastoral contrast.
The farmer, for all his city upbringing, turns out to be less
sophisticated than his hired hand in that his words have no
special significance beneath their outward meaning. He
has just said what he thought in a simple and direct way.
By contrast, the Yankee has a far more complicated mind.
For him, even the most casual remarks are the medium for
hinting at attitudes and judgments. He weighs and interprets every word.

Such hypersensitivity is not as absurd as it seems. The
outsider may take it as a quaint local trait, but as the poem
goes on to show, it is actually the outgrowth of a very
highly developed ethical sense. The farmer has unknow-
ingly challenged the Yankee's most precious convictions
—his belief that a man of honor will take pride in his
work, that any hint he is not doing his best is therefore a
slur upon his integrity, that no one has a right to question
another's character in this manner. The code as a way of

communicating serves to demonstrate the high idealism of the code as an ethic. The fact that the Yankee is so sensitive to the least questioning of his honor shows the loftiness of his ideals. Furthermore, this subtlety is an essential part of the Yankee ethic, for the elaborate method of communicating is the means for keeping the ethic from being compromised.

With this in mind, let us turn to the main narrative, the hired man's explanation of regional ways. His theme is the Yankee's pride in his work. "The hand that knows his business won't be told/ To do work better or faster," he grimly asserts. To illustrate the point, he tells the story of how he once took revenge on a farmer who challenged his honor by urging him to work harder. The man, whose name was Sanders, was one of those bosses who can never resist the temptation to drive their men. Sanders set himself up as an example of tireless industry. He was always busy at something, as if to reproach his men for their laziness, and he would stoop rather far to "encourage" them.

> Them that he couldn't lead he'd get behind
> And drive, the way you can, you know, in mowing—
> Keep at their heels and threaten to mow their legs off.

The narrator had been watching this for some time, and made up his mind to resist. Finally, one day, the crisis came. He and Sanders had brought in a load of hay to the barn, and as he stood in the wagon about to unload it, Sanders, down in the bay, could not quite resist shouting up one extra bit of encouragement. "Let her come!" he roared—

> Thinks I, D'ye mean it? "What was that you said?"
> I asked out loud, so's there'd be no mistake,
> "Did you say, Let her come?" "Yes, let her come."
> He said it over, but he said it softer.
> Never you say a thing like that to a man,
> Not if he values what he is.

Enraged, the narrator unloaded the entire wagonload of hay on Sanders' head. But this is not a murder story. The other hands, when they searched the hay, were unable to find the victim's body. Somehow he had managed to escape and was later discovered nursing his pride by the kitchen stove, "the hottest day that summer."

The story is slight, and, in one sense, its meaning is obvious. It may seem simply to dramatize the rural Yankee's exaggerated sense of self-respect. But its freshness and vitality survive the test of many rereadings. The more one considers it, the more one becomes aware that the lesson the Yankee hired man intends—that is, the lesson about the Yankee attitude toward work—is only a part of the total meaning. His lesson is, of course important, but the way he tells his story brings into the poem other complexly interwoven strands of meaning. These, I think, can best be appreciated by returning to the poem's basic purpose—its exposition of the Yankee code. As we have seen, the code is something far more intricate than a mere set of rules. It is the whole regional system of values as it actually exists in living people, embodied in their way of thought. What Frost means to portray is not simply the Yankee's belief in the independence of the individual or pride in one's work, but the way these beliefs are realized in his thought process. The code is a common ground, and because of this it functions as a means of communicating. We see that Sanders can say very harsh things indeed through what seem like the most commonplace remarks. And the narrator's response to them shows how wide is the leap of inference from what is said to what is implied. The effect is to dramatize in a very striking way the nuances and indirections through which the Yankees communicate.

All this heads up in the simple words, "Let her come." To the outsider, these words seem innocent enough; to the

Yankee they are a direct challenge, one which so enrages him that he is ready to murder Sanders. Although his anger is extreme, he is, in a sense, right. He has not misread Sanders' words, for Sanders is a Yankee too and understands the code. Indeed, at the end we see that Sanders shares the same moral sense as well as the same habit of mind. "Did he discharge you?" the farmer asks. "Discharge me? No! He knew I did just right."

It would falsify the poem to ignore the fact that this is a comic story. While the code embodies deep convictions, Frost's portrayal of it is more than a little humorous. One cannot help being amused by the discrepancy between the trivial details and the weight of significance the Yankees find in them. At one point, the narrator explains:

> They realized from the way I swabbed my neck
> More than was needed something must be up.

Such bits of humor result from the fundamental irony of pastoral. Crude, simple things take on a comic seriousness just as the humble and commonplace take on an unexpected dignity. In the end, if we smile at the Yankee field hand for making so much of such a harmless phrase as "Let her come," we are more than a little inclined to admire him for his high sense of the dignity of work.

By making the style function symbolically, Frost achieves a unity between the subject and the way it is presented. In "The Code," the paradox we have noted in the Yankee way of thought also underlies the general meaning of the poem. What is the significance of the anecdote which this poem presents? The question may best be answered by defining one's attitude toward the narrator at the very end. And this is not likely to be a simple attitude. In some respects the narrator's punishment of Sanders appears right; when looked at from another point of view, it seems rather harsh. At the end, he admits the intent to murder:

"I went about to kill him fair enough." "You took an awk-
ward way," the farmer replies, and however much we ap-
plaud the narrator for defending his rights, it is hard to
agree that he would have been justified in murdering
Sanders just because the man had insulted him. We and
the city-bred farmer are civilized and have more moderate
ways of handling such grievances. On the other hand,
doesn't such moderation reveal a willingness to compromise our ideals? The Yankee's bloody intention suggests he
has a higher loyalty to his. One disapproves of his attempt
in the same way that one disapproves of the duelist's way
of defending his honor. In both cases, the code seems
primitive yet at the same time evidence of a higher valua-
tion of man's personal integrity than can be found in the
urban world. There is the typical ironic effect of pastoral
in the idea that the chivalry which lived by a code of
honor only survives among back-country farmers.

The more one considers the narrator, the more ambiguous his character seems. He may be friendly to the farmer,
good-humored, and amusing, but there is a disconcerting
callousness in him too. His dry manner has something
cold-blooded about it, as when he explains:

> I guess they thought I'd spiked him in the temple
> Before I buried him, or I couldn't have managed.

And there is a glint of ferocity in his description of
Sanders overwhelmed by the hay: "He squeaked like a
squeezed rat."

Are we to laugh or shudder? One's final attitude is apt
to be a balance of contrary feelings. Though the reader
may see the hired man as an admirable figure, he will also
share the city-bred farmer's misgivings. There is, of course,
no certain answer as to whether the hired man's revenge
was right or wrong. This ambiguity suits well with the
poem's general intent, which is not to point a lesson, but

to present a picture of the regional world in all its complexity. Any clear decision would commit Frost to accept either the Yankee point of view or the more sophisticated standard of the city-bred farmer, and this is what he is most anxious to avoid. He wishes to maintain the integrity of both, to let them act as a commentary upon one another, and in this way to reveal the full range of meaning inherent in the story. The style is one of the most important means for creating this kind of contrast. Because it is a part of the Yankee code and represents the code as a whole, the style becomes "a constant symbol" of Frost's New England. In it, as well as through it, we see the essential nature of the Yankee mind.

CHAPTER 4

PASTORALISM AND THE DRAMATIC

The poetic design we see "writ large" in the pastorals is discernible to a greater or lesser extent in the great bulk of the poet's other work. Pastoralism may, therefore, be thought of as occupying a central position whence one can move outward in several directions to explore other areas of his poetry. The present chapter and the one which follows are intended as an exploration of this sort. Of course, we cannot hope to consider every aspect of Frost's poetry, nor will it be necessary to do so in order to appreciate the importance of his pastoralism. Instead of conducting a general survey, therefore, I will discuss two major aspects of Frost which illustrate the extent to which pastoralism has influenced the structure of his nonpastoral poetry. This chapter deals with Frost's dramatic poems, while the following examines his role as a nature poet.

1

Frost's remarkable dramatic gift has been so often acclaimed that the average reader today may be inclined to take it for granted. His interest in drama is well known.

Over and over again, both in his public talks and in his prefaces, he has emphasized the importance of the dramatic element in literature, and as a practicing poet he has produced, not only two one-act plays, but two long poems—"A Masque of Reason" and "A Masque of Mercy"—in dramatic form.[1] In view of all this, it is of some significance that Frost has never attempted a full-fledged play. The two one-acters are slight affairs indeed, and the masques, though considerable poetic achievements, are not actual dramas. The truth is that his reputation as a dramatic poet rests, not on his plays and masques, but on his dramatic lyrics, his monologues, dialogues, and little playlet-like scenes set within a narrative framework.

If Frost's poetry is dramatic, it is dramatic in a special way. It will therefore be best to set aside for the moment the prevalent idea that his dramatic poems are simply plays constructed on a very modest scale. Instead, let us consider of just what his dramatic poetry consists and in what relation it stands to the pastoralism with which we have become familiar in the Yankee poems. In this way, both the source and the limitations of his dramatic gift will become apparent.

Roughly a score of Frost's poems may be considered essentially dramatic. If these were classified strictly according to their form, it would be found that only two are dramatic monologues in the usual sense and only three are what might be called dramatic dialogues. The bulk of Frost's dramatic poems, and this includes almost all of the really familiar ones, would be technically disqualified, for they are really monologues and dialogues presented within a more or less elaborate narrative framework. This is a fact of some importance; it shows that the best of Frost's drama comes to us through the mediation of a nar-

1. The plays are *The Cow's in the Corn* (Gaylordsville, 1929), in verse; and *A Way Out*, in prose.

rator. In some of these poems, only faint traces of the narrative framework are discernible in stage directions or bits of description interspersed here and there through the dramatic speech. In others, however, the narrator intervenes frequently and at some length to set the mood of the scene and describe the shifting emotions of his characters. But whether the dramatic passages are richly augmented with description, as in "The Death of the Hired Man," or the narrative element is sparse, as in "The Witch of Coös," Frost's dependence upon the narrative form indicates that his dramatic works are not far removed from his other poems and have grown out of the same kind of poetic thought.

How then are we to distinguish the dramatic pieces from the rest? Many seem to occupy a borderland between dramatic and narrative or dramatic and lyric. For example, "The Death of the Hired Man," which is generally considered a dramatic poem, not only contains much lyric description, but is mainly taken up with past events. Is this poem really distinguishable from such nondramatic poems as "The Code," in which a dramatic incident provides the starting point for a long narrative monologue? Another case in point is the poem called "Blueberries." This is written in the form of a dramatic dialogue, and it lacks the usual narrative frame, yet its total effect seems lyric rather than dramatic.

It soon becomes clear that the difference between Frost's dramatic and nondramatic poetry is not merely a matter of form. "Blueberries," though dramatic in form, is not a dramatic poem, while "The Death of the Hired Man," despite its long narrative portions, is. Whether the lines are attributed directly to the characters or come to us via a narrator is not nearly so important as whether or not the portrayal of action (either physical or psychological) is predominant. The only valid way of distinguishing the dramatic poems is by their primary emphasis on *action felt to be happening in the present*. The difference between narrative and lyric on the one hand and dramatic on the other is the difference between events recollected and events seen in the present. The action in the dramatic poems has immediacy—we seem to see the events acted out before us. Where the action has this immediacy, the narrative elements will be clearly secondary; retrospection will give way to a sense of present experience.

There are, however, different kinds of action and hence differing forms of drama. In some of Frost's dramatic pieces what the characters do and say is of great import, so that we may see serious consequences looming in their future lives; in others the action is nothing more than a good conversation, philosophic or simply amusing. For example, both "Home Burial" and "West-Running Brook" are dramatic, yet anyone who will take the trouble to compare these poems will see that they are quite different. "Home Burial" reveals the characters in a moment of supreme crisis, while in "West-Running Brook" we glimpse what is merely a typical moment in the characters' lives. Because of this variety it will be useful to consider the types of poetic form in which Frost's dramatic sense expresses itself. This will serve to show the connection between his dramatic verse and the rest of his work. We will see that the dramatic poems form a continuum extending from the most intensely impassioned speech downward into conversation, and from this in turn into anecdote and reminiscence, that is, pure narrative and lyric.

Frost's dramatic poems fall into five general groupings. The purpose of the following classification is not to make exact distinctions but to class each poem according to its essential form.

I DRAMATIC DIALOGUES

The Death of the Hired Man
Home Burial
The Fear
The Self-Seeker
In the Home Stretch
Snow
The Generations of Men

II DRAMATIC MONOLOGUES

A Servant to Servants
The Witch of Coös
The Pauper Witch of Grafton

III PASTORAL DIALOGUES

The Mountain
A Hundred Collars
Blueberries

IV PHILOSOPHIC DIALOGUES

A Fountain, a Bottle, a Donkey's
    Ears, and Some Books
West-Running Brook
Build Soil
From Plane to Plane
A Literate Farmer and the Planet
    Venus

V NARRATIVE MONOLOGUES

The Bonfire
The Housekeeper

The terms I have used call for some explanation, and thus we may best begin by considering the nature of each group.

Dramatic dialogues. The poems in this class represent Frost's most thoroughly dramatic work. In them the action is the main interest. They are, in effect, little plays, presenting—though perhaps very simply—what Aristotle defines as drama, that is, a single and complete action.

"The Death of the Hired Man" illustrates nicely Frost's skill in building a complete plot within the compass of a short poem. The hired man does not appear in the poem, but he is nevertheless the main character. His death is the center of the action, and the poet gradually unfolds the meaning of this event through the successive perceptions of Mary and Warren, the married couple to whose house the hired man has returned to die. The *agon* or dramatic struggle consists in Mary's efforts to persuade her husband that they must accept their obligation to help the hired man in his broken and useless old age. Warren, who is more tied to practical considerations, objects that the old man is unreliable and will be of little use around the farm. He can see no reason why he should take back the man who again and again has hired himself to work on their farm only to leave them for higher pay just at harvest time when he was most needed. Warren has not seen the hired man since his return, and he does not know that he is close to death. But what is more important, he does not understand the hired man's character. The movement of the action is the revealing of the hired man's true self as Mary strives to make her husband understand the fundamental self-respect which lies beneath his plea for their help. In the struggle between Mary's sympathy and Warren's practical objections each additional argument provides fresh information. As Mary's understanding gradually wins Warren over to a more compassionate view, the hired man is revealed in clearer and clearer outline. The final truth about his personality is his imminent death. When we learn of this at the end of the poem, it comes as the inevitable culmination of all that we have come to know about him. For it is in the fact of his death that we see the basis of his character and life, the high idealism which would not allow him to throw himself on the charity of relatives, but led him instead to seek work at Warren's farm in order that he might at least maintain the fiction of his independence. His self-respect has been the essence of his life, and now that this self-respect can exist only as a charitable fiction, his life is in the truest sense ended.

This is, perhaps, the most perfectly shaped of Frost's dramatic pieces, but the same completeness and unity of action may be found in all the dramatic dialogues. Not all of them, of course, are fully successful. I would not rank "The Self-Seeker" or "Snow" among Frost's best poems. But all reveal the same basic form. In reading any one of them, one senses that something of importance is taking place, and that Frost has worked to make every detail in the poem contribute to the fulfillment of this event.

Of course the dramatic event is not always a physical action. Drama is essentially psychological, and in some of Frost's finest dramatic poems the action is no less complete because it consists simply in a change of attitude or the attainment of a new perception. Thus, for example, the young wife of "Home Burial" is gradually persuaded to bring out into the open her sorrow over the death of her first-born infant. By expressing her feelings in words, she comes to understand them. She imagines that she must give over her life to her sorrow for the child's death. She refuses to accept her husband's love, because he seems to have accepted this death with callous indifference. She cannot understand how he could have buried the child himself. She is horrified that he should have come into the kitchen with his boots muddy from the earth of the grave and left the shovel in the entry way. In the days since then she has cut herself off from him, erecting a barrier of hatred between them. Now as her husband forces her to talk of these things she at last comes to see that her grief and resentment result from the pain of discovering that human nature is limited and cannot sacrifice everything to sorrow. When she finally asserts, half hysterically, that she will not compromise her grief by returning to normal life, one senses that she herself sees the absurdity of her attitude. Her husband's kind yet firm reasonableness indicates that though she still suffers from the excess of grief, the crisis is now past and she will eventually be led back to life.

Dramatic monologues. Only two of Frost's poems—"A Servant to Servants" and "The Pauper Witch of Grafton" —are so written that every word is presented as the speech of a single character. Strictly speaking, these are his only dramatic monologues, yet such a narrow view is not realistic. It is the general spirit of the poem rather than the technical matter of how many lines are attributed to the main character that counts. In their basic form, several of Frost's poems are really dramatic monologues, since in them the drama takes place within a single character. This becomes clear when we compare these poems with the dramatic dialogues. In a dialogue, interest is focused upon the relations between two or more persons, and we see the action in terms of the effect they have upon each other, in the give-and-take which results when people speak their minds to one another. In the monologue, on the other hand, attention is centered exclusively upon the psychological change within the single major character. Here the situation, including the characters who listen to him and may occasionally speak, is arranged in such a way that the central personality is shown in the clearest possible light. This distinction may seem too obvious to mention, but it is important to keep in mind, for the difference in the focus of interest makes for a difference in the poetic form itself.

In the dramatic monologues the action is always psychological. The drama consists either in self-revelation or self-realization, the latter being the more powerful kind of action. "The Pauper Witch of Grafton" illustrates the drama of self-revelation. In this poem, the old witch merely casts light into the hidden corners of her personality for the benefit of her audience. It is clear that she understands her own nature as well at the beginning of her monologue as at the end. We neither see her in a moment of crisis in her life nor in the act of making an important decision; rather, the action consists in the gradual unfolding of her secret as we come to recognize the sexual basis of her eccentricity.

"The Witch of Coös," on the other hand, is more intensely dramatic, for here we are shown the main character at the crucial moment in which she gains a new insight into her past life. Her witchcraft grows from the neurotic

projection of sexual guilt. The skeleton, which, as she re-
lates, once climbed up from its grave in the cellar to the
attic and was then nailed in forever, is the imagined ghost
of the lover her husband killed to avenge her adultery.
After she had helped her husband bury the man in the
cellar, the phantasy of the walking skeleton was created
by suppressed guilt and her ambivalent attitudes toward
both husband and lover. Now, years later, as she recounts
the story to her visitor, we see that her superstitious imagination has at last completed its work. By objectifying her
inner confusion it has made the truth bearable. At the end
of the poem, the woman finds that time has brought her
the resignation to look squarely at her past life, and for
the first time she confesses the truth.

The action, then, takes place entirely within the main
character. The subordinate role of the other characters is
clearly indicative of this. The narrator, who presents
the poem as an experience he had when he spent a night at
a lonely farmhouse, speaks only at the beginning and end.
He serves merely as an audience to whom the witch can tell
her curious story. But there is also her son, aged about
forty, whose speech indicates he is mentally retarded. It
is he who urges his mother to talk, first by boasting of her
spiritual powers and then by leading her to tell of the
bones "up attic." His role is even more important at the
end, when his naive remarks drive her to confess:

SON.   We never could find out whose bones they were.
MOTHER.   Yes, we could too, son. Tell the truth for
    once. . . .

Son looks surprised to see me end a lie
We'd kept all these years between ourselves
So as to have it ready for outsiders.
But tonight I don't care enough to lie—

True, the witch's story would not be possible without the narrator and the son. But there is no real action between the characters. The narrator and the son merely provide the occasion for the main character's recognition of herself. A similar self-realization is the essence of another beautifully constructed monologue, "A Servant to Servants." Here we see a farm wife, overworked, distraught, and fearful of relapsing into hereditary insanity, as she comes to realize the extent of her lonely desperation.

There is a distinct difference between the dramatic dialogues and monologues and the poems of groups III, IV and V. The poems I have called pastoral, philosophic, and narrative are also concerned with action, but in them the action is subordinated to some ulterior purpose. It is used to typify a person or situation, to dramatize some philosophic idea, or to occasion a narrative.

Pastoral dialogues. In the pastoral dialogues the action is still of much interest, but one senses that it is less important than in the poems discussed above. When one compares such a poem as "A Hundred Collars" with "The Death of the Hired Man," the difference in degree of dramatic intensity is apparent. The reader may feel that the former poem makes a less powerful appeal to the emotions simply because it is concerned with a less serious subject. But this is not so. The poem is less dramatic because the action it presents is merely a means of illustrating a social relationship. The subject is not the events themselves, but a situation which the events serve to define.

"A Hundred Collars" records the conversation between two men forced to spend the night together in a dingy, railroad-junction hotel up New Hampshire way. One, Doctor Magoon, is a distinguished scholar and college teacher. On a visit to the family homestead at Lancaster, he has been delayed by bad train connections and so finds himself forced to share a room with a stranger. His companion for the night, Lafe (short for Lafayette), is a good-humored but somewhat vulgar traveling bill collector who spends his days moving about the countryside for a local newspaper.

Doctor Magoon would like to think of himself as a democratic person, but he has long since lost touch with the common people. The shabby Mr. Lafayette seems to him a suspicious character, a thief perhaps, or even, he fearfully imagines, a cutthroat. His tactless nervousness soon makes this clear to Lafe, but Lafe is magnanimous enough to ignore the affront. He tries to reassure Doctor Magoon, first by showing that he himself has more money to risk by trusting the doctor than the doctor could lose by trusting him, and then by offering him a drink from his flask. In his sociable way Lafe rambles on about politics, the outlying farms he visits, and the beauty of the country-side. The contrast between Lafe's easygoing disposition and the scholar's squeamishness is the essence of the dramatic situation. The gulf separating the two men is obvious, and Lafe's generous efforts to bridge it by offering to send Doctor Magoon a great many old but perfectly good collars which he has outgrown only serve to make the situation more hopeless.

That it deals with a situation, rather than an action, explains why "A Hundred Collars" falls short of the dramatic intensity of "The Death of the Hired Man." Its theme is no less dignified or important: what subject is richer in dramatic potential than the misunderstandings which isolate human beings from one another? Yet we do not see this subject in a single action which grows from past events to future consequences. The characters remain exactly the same throughout, and in the end, though much has been said, it is clear that nothing has happened. True, there are events in the poem—the characters exchange opinions and their feelings are revealed. But all this is merely a patchwork of little incidents; it does not constitute a dramatic action.

Indeed, the basic intent of the poem makes a true dramatic action impossible. For "A Hundred Collars" and the other pastoral dialogues are not mainly concerned either with character study or with the portrayal of events. In these poems Frost's real subject is the contrast between two worlds. Drama is subordinated to the purposes of pastoral; it becomes the means for exploring rural New England by holding it up for comparison with modern urban life. Those who take "A Hundred Collars" as a mere character sketch are apt to miss the true richness of this poem. For while Lafe emerges as a distinct person, what makes his character interesting is the way of life it embodies. He represents the solid Yankee virtues, the common sense, the shrewd perceptiveness, and subtle tact which raise New England above the rest of the country. And these are revealed dramatically through the juxtaposition of Lafe and Doctor Magoon, the urban sophisticate, whose superior education and respectability mask a very ordinary mind.

The characters, then, are representatives, and for this very reason the pastoral dialogue can only be dramatic to a limited degree. Since each man typifies a way of life—something which persists without change through the years—the relationship between them must be static. The line of development is not the evolution of a dramatic action, but the exposition of a set state of affairs. Just as "The Death of the Hired Man" resembles a one-act play, "A Hundred Collars" and the other pastoral dialogues correspond to the theatrical form known as the tableau.

The reason for calling these poems *pastoral* dialogues should now be clear. While many of Frost's other dramatic poems are also true pastorals in that they are set within the regional context, only the poems of this group have a dramatic form which is dictated by the basic structure of pastoral. This is so because in them rural New England itself is the main subject. As a subject regionalism offers strong theatrical contrasts, but it also imposes limitations upon drama, for it leads to a drama of situations rather than events.

Philosophic dialogues. The poems of this group are dramatic in a still more limited way. In them, the action dramatizes, not a situation, but a philosophical idea. The form of these poems is very reminiscent of certain traditional eclogues. The speakers discuss a thesis, and the dramatic action serves merely to illustrate the main theme. In "From Plane to Plane," for example, we listen to the conversation of two men, an old Yankee field hand and a youth on vacation from college, as they work side by side in a cornfield along the Connecticut valley. Their talk turns on the subject of work. Pike, the field hand, claims that men whose occupations are more "respectable" do not work nearly so hard as the manual laborer. To prove his point he cites the country doctor, who can be seen journeying across the flat countryside in his buggy:

> Nowhere but on the Bradford Interval
> By the Connecticut could anyone
> Have stayed in sight so long as an example.

Dick takes the other side of the argument. The doctor, he replies, is just taking a necessary rest. He contends that every man, if he is to maintain his integrity, must detach himself now and then from the rest of the world. Even for Pike this is true; he always walks back the length of the field after he has hoed a row of corn before beginning another. Pike seems to agree. He will not admit a resemblance to the doctor, but it is his thesis that "A man has got to keep his extrication." His little rest at the end of each row of corn is an example, and he mentions the sun's withdrawal southward after summer begins as a like instance in nature.

One can see in this poem that the dramatic medium offers Frost several advantages. He is able to present the theme interestingly and naturally through the rapid interplay of ideas in the lightly bantering conversation of the two men, so that it is viewed from a number of angles, but what is more important, the dramatic form allows for the portrayal of action which illustrates the theme. The occasion for their argument is the friendly rivalry between them. Beneath their casual conversation there is a kind of dramatic struggle. Just as both agree that "extrication" is necessary for every man, so too as they talk together they both strive to maintain their sense of personal independence. To do this, neither can compromise his position by yielding too much in the argument, and neither will attempt to impose his opinions upon the other. Their attitude is conciliatory; they search for a common ground. But this is not an easy task—it takes all of their tact and resourcefulness to maintain the balance of friendliness and independence. The argument is an act of friendship symbolized by the work they perform as they talk:

> They were both bent on scuffling up
> Alluvium so pure that when a blade
> To their surprise rang once on stone all day
> Each tried to be the first at getting in
> A superstitious cry for farmer's luck—
> A rivalry that made them both feel kinder.

Their way of reaching an agreement which preserves for each his "extrication" dramatizes the poem's theme. Pike, without seeming to yield too much, concedes that the doctor

> may be some good in a manner of speaking.
> I own he does look busy when the sun
> Is in the sign of Sickness in the winter.

Dick, in return wishing "to let Pike seem to have the palm/ With grace and not too formal a surrender," finds a ground for agreement in the idea that "extrication" is necessary not only as a respite from work but also as a way of modestly escaping the thanks of those one has obliged. This idea is couched ingeniously in the form of a rather indirect compliment, which saves them both embarrassment and expresses thanks without seeming to. In answer, Pike points out that the desire to show gratitude is, after all, a weakness—like having to have a Santa Claus to thank at Christmas. Throughout, neither yields too much to his companion, and yet the old field hand and the college youth, though separated by so much, discover the basis for friendship in the mutual respect which allows each to maintain his independence. There is a good deal of dramatic interest in the process by which Pike and Dick preserve the balance of equality, but it is perfectly clear that this action is not the main subject. Here it is the thesis which counts, and the action merely serves to illustrate what is said.

The same use of dramatic action may be found in "West-Running Brook," the title poem of the volume which Frost published in 1928. While this poem lacks the pastoral quality of "From Plane to Plane," it is fundamentally similar in design. The thematic idea of "West-Running Brook" is that life, whether in its most primitive form or in man himself, originates in an instinct of resistance, in a thrusting backward against the current of decay—

> The universal cataract of death
> That spends to nothingness—and unresisted,

> Save by some strange resistance in itself,
> Not just a swerving, but a throwing back,
> As if regret were in it and were sacred.
> It has this throwing backward on itself
> So that the fall of most of it is always
> Raising a little, sending up a little. . . .
>
> It is this backward motion toward the source,
> Against the stream, that most we see ourselves in,
> The tribute of the current to the source.
> It is from this in nature we are from.
> It is most us.

Both the setting and the relationship between the two speakers are accommodated to this core idea. The poem is cast in the form of a conversation between a young married couple, who are out for a country stroll and have stopped to look at West-Running Brook. This brook, which runs west in a region where all streams are supposed to flow eastward to the sea, seems to the couple the very spirit of contrariness. Then they notice a small white wave caused by something beneath the water. It rises against the current, endlessly riding the black water, "Not gaining but not losing, like a bird." This sets the man to musing. He sees the contrary brook and the contrary wave as symbols of life itself. They represent, he says, the vital force, the "backward motion toward the source," and he goes on to develop this idea at some length.

While the philosophic motif holds the center of interest throughout, the dramatic framework of the poem is of some importance. The action, like the setting, symbolizes the central idea. The conversation is an argument between lovers, and the poet so arranges it as to suggest that disagreement of a sort is fundamental to their love. At the beginning the woman remarks:

It must be the brook
Can trust itself to go by contraries
The way I can with you—and you with me.

This sets the tone of the whole poem. It is at once a dispute and a love-making in which endearment takes the form of playful banter. The closing lines show especially well how skillfully Frost has molded the dialogue into a dramatic illustration of his theme:

'It is from this in nature we are from.
It is most us.'
                    'Today will be the day
You said so.'
                    'No, today will be the day
You said the brook was called West-Running Brook.'
'Today will be the day of what we both said.'

Narrative monologues. But one group of poems remains, and this demands the least attention in that it comprises the least dramatic type, that in which drama fades into pure narrative. I have listed only two poems in this category, but one might include others—"The Code" or "The Black Cottage," for example. Indeed, one cannot be sure just where to draw the line, since the only clear difference between these poems and other narratives is in the matter of speech attribution. The action is of little importance; at most it merely provides the occasion for the telling of a story. Since the monologuist may have an interlocutor who says a word or two, and since there is always the possibility of stage business of some sort, poems of this type may seem closer to drama than they actually are. They present past events discussed or narrated in character, and the monologue form serves mainly to define the point of view from which the story is told.

"The Housekeeper" is a poem of this sort. The "I" here

is a secondary character, and, aside from the few brief questions he asks, the entire poem is presented as the speech of an elderly housekeeper. The story she tells is of her daughter Estelle's elopement. Estelle had lived for many years with the man for whom her mother keeps house, but as time went by she became increasingly dissatisfied with her life as a common-law wife, until at last, on the previous day, she has run off with another man— one who has offered to marry her. The main interest of the story lies in the discovery of Estelle's motives. As her mother fills in more and more details of Estelle's past life, we gradually realize that the real reason for her flight is neither the shame nor the hard usage a woman in her position must suffer, but simply resentment. She has been hurt by the careless insensitivity of the man who could never quite make up his mind to marry her. At the end of the poem the foresaken man returns home, having just learned the news, and the housekeeper sums up her story by dismissing him as a "dreadful fool." Because the housekeeper's story is set in the midst of agitating events, and because she is in a sense "breaking the news," the poem has an atmosphere of dramatic excitement. But nothing of importance happens while the housekeeper speaks. The real action is in the past, and the poem is dramatic only in the sense that the story is told in character.

2

I have considered the various forms of action in Frost's dramatic verse in some detail because it seems to me important to recognize that his dramatic writing is an outgrowth of his most characteristic work. His art is essentially narrative and lyric rather than dramatic. This explains why he has never attempted a major work for the theatre. Not that his sense of drama is inferior, but in him the instincts of a playwright have never been dominant. Even his most dramatic poems, "The Death of the Hired Man" and "The Witch of Coös," are still within the realm of storytelling. One sees the closeness to narrative in his habitual use of the frame story. Nevertheless, he has a strong dramatic tendency, and this, I would suggest, results from the very nature of his poetic vision. The five groups of poems we have examined reveal a gentle gradation from narrative poetry to a kind of verse which stops just short of theatrical form. This transition makes it clear that the dramatic poems are not something different but represent an extension of Frost's normal methods as a poet.

The most important source of his dramatic impulse is the basic design of pastoral. Pastoral is always potentially dramatic, for it depends upon a perspective of sharp contrasts. It portrays the town in terms of the country, the rich in terms of the poor, the complex in terms of the simple, and thus it works through a sense of conflict, through opposed points of view, through the ironic difference between people and classes. The very subject matter of pastoral produces the tensions suitable for drama. The traditional eclogues from Theocritus to Pope are more often dialogues than reflective poems, more often monologues than lyrics. Even the pastoral lament is largely dramatic; it is almost always a song presented in a singing contest or a lover's complaint sung for the benefit of the swain's confidant. The debate, the conversation between lovers, and the singing contest are among the commonest forms of pastoral, and all of them involve dialogue and some degree of dramatic action. The flourishing pastoral drama of the Renaissance is only a further development of the drama inherent in all pastoral. As Empson has pointed out, the pastoral parallel between high and low life fitted perfectly with the Elizabethan double plot.[2] In the masque, the same

2. *English Pastoral Poetry*, pp. 27–86.

contrast could serve the purposes of allegory. For Frost, then, pastoral led to dramatic verse. He had only to focus the contrasts inherent in his regional art in fictional characters to move from narrative to dramatic poetry.

Frost has said that he first heard the "sound of speech" in poetry while reading one of Virgil's eclogues. I do not know whether it was the first eclogue or not, but it might well have been, for in "Build Soil: A Political Pastoral" he has written a parody of Virgil's poem. In Frost as in Virgil, Tityrus and Meliboeus are an aged poet and a distressed young farmer, and they discuss the farm problem of the great depression much as their ancient counterparts the economic plight of farmers in Latium.[3] Frost transforms the Virgilian nostalgia for country life into a manifesto for regionalist self-reliance.[4] The poem is not one of his best, but it is important, because it indicates not only the poet's consciousness of his ties with the pastoral tradition but the link between pastoral, the sound of speech, and dramatic poetry.

In Frost's verse, all three stem from the same conception of poetry. A passage from the preface to his one-act play, *A Way Out,* shows that Frost considers some measure of drama necessary to all creative writing:

3. Like Frost's, Virgil's poem is, of course, allegorical, though there is some disagreement as to the degree of importance and the definiteness of the allusions. The traditional interpretation of modern scholarship sees the poem as a reflection of an incident in Virgil's life, Tityrus corresponding to Virgil and the youth he praises to Octavius. For a discussion of the allegorical problem, see Edward K. Rand, *The Magical Art of Vergil* (Cambridge, Mass., 1931), pp. 145–52.

4. Lawrance Thompson, in *Fire and Ice: The Art and Thought of Robert Frost* (New York, 1942), notes the parallel to Virgil's First Eclogue. See pp. 153–4 of his text. He also suggests that Frost intended a reference to the Fourth Eclogue, but his evidence has to do with the circumstances in which Frost composed his poem rather than any similarity between the two poems. One can scarcely view "Build Soil" as a treatment of Virgil's golden age theme, yet this is the only link between the two poems Thompson suggests.

Everything written is as good as it is dramatic. It need not declare itself in form, but it is drama or nothing. A least lyric alone may have a hard time, but it can make a beginning, and lyric will be piled on lyric *till all are easily heard as sung or spoken by a person in a scene—in character, in a setting.* By whom, where and when is the question. By a dreamer of the better world out in a storm in Autumn; by a lover under a window at night.[5]

Frost is here speaking of all poetry, but what he says applies with especial force to his own. For in the kind of poetry he writes the persona and the dramatic situation are developed far beyond their rudimentary form in the average lyric or narrative. We have already noted the importance of the Yankee speaker in the pastorals as a symbol of the rural world. Such a use of the speaker is a simple form of dramatizing. So too is the technique of recording the sound of speech. Dramatic writing required only a slight shift of emphasis: the Yankee speaker was already there, and all that was needed to transform him into the monologuist was a set of urgent circumstances. So far as form is concerned, the difference between a full-fledged monologue such as "The Witch of Coös" and a lyric like "Stopping by Woods on a Snowy Evening" consists merely in the degree to which the speaker's circumstances are developed.

Nor is the movement from monologue to dialogue a decisive step. Pastoral by its very nature assumes an audience, since it is concerned with explaining and interpreting rural life to those who live in a quite different milieu. The sense of audience is always very strong in Frost's work. His lyrics have the quality of speech addressed to someone

5. p. [iii]. The italics are mine.

in particular, but even when the poem is directed to the general reading public rather than an imaginary interlocutor, which is the case in "New Hampshire," the dramatic dimension is important. The success of "New Hampshire" depends upon the fact that the audience does not know regional life and must be told. In "The Code," the audience emerges as a person, the town-bred farmer to whom the old Yankee field hand explains rural ways. From this interlocutor it is only a step to Warren, a fully dramatic character with whom the main character, Mary, must struggle in her effort to make him understand the secret nobility of the hired man. Dialogue is common in the old pastorals, and Frost's pastoralism inevitably encouraged his use of it.

Pastoralism fostered his dramatic talent in still another way. It offered not only characters and action, but a stage. Dramatic action requires an ordered and complete setting. The events of a play take on meaning from the world in which we see them, and they can only be meaningful to the extent that the stage on which they are acted out is fully conceived. The setting, then, must be more than mere acting space; it must represent a total conception of reality, one which brings together an implied set of ideas as to the nature of being, a social order, and a system of values in a single scheme of things. Frost's rural world is such a setting. For him, the transition to dramatic poetry from other forms required merely a turning from retrospection to present action.

His impulse to philosophize is very strong, and this too has encouraged his tendency to drama. Frost the philosopher is quite different from other poets who like to deal in general ideas. In Wordsworth, Tennyson, Eliot, or Stevens, for example, the speaker is characteristically portrayed as a solitary figure wrapped in his own thought; in consequence, his tone tends to be either meditative or rhapsodic. In Frost's philosophic poems, on the other hand, the speaker's manner is nearly always conversational. Whether he exchanges opinions with another character, as in "West-Running Brook," or whether he alone speaks, the discussion of ideas is directed to others and is, therefore, speech rather than unspoken thought translated into words. I can think of no poet in English after Pope who has succeeded so well in treating ideas in the medium of conversation. Those who have heard Frost will be quick to see that his conception of the philosophic poem springs from his own speaking gift. He is both a brilliant conversationalist and a professional lecturer of exceptional talent. His effectiveness before audiences results from his conception of the lecture as a poetic form in which the speaker develops his ideas spontaneously through a kind of one-way conversation with his listeners. His method is to start from some general idea, elaborating it through a score of speculations disguised as informal comments. His talks are exciting, because he gives his listeners the sense of witnessing poetry in the very process of creation, and it is probable that many more poems than we know of first took shape in the lecture hall. I shall cite but one example. In February, 1931, he gave a talk at Amherst in which, speaking of the internationalists of that time, he said:

I should want to say to anyone like that: "Look! First I want to be a person. And I want you to be a person, and then we can be as interpersonal as you please. . . . But, first of all you have got to have the personality. First of all, you have got to have the nations and then they can be as international as they please with each other."

I should like to use another metaphor on them. I want my palette, if I am a painter, I want my palette on my thumb or on my chair, all clean, pure, separate colors. Then I will do the mixing on the canvas. The canvas is where the work of art is, where we make the conquest. But we want the nations all separate, pure, distinct, things as separate as we can make them; and then in our thoughts, in our arts, and so on, we can do what we please about it.[6]

In "Build Soil," which the poet read at Columbia University some fifteen months later, this passage emerges as poetry:

> But long before I'm interpersonal
> Away 'way down inside I'm personal.
> Just so before we're international
> We're national and act as nationals.
> The colors are kept unmixed on the palette,
> Or better on dish plates all around the room,
> So the effect when they are mixed on canvas
> May seem almost exclusively designed.
> Some minds are so confounded intermental
> They remind me of pictures on a palette.

The closeness of Frost the lecturer and Frost the philosophic poet is significant. The arts by which he surmounts the formality of the lecture hall to create the direct and informal relation with his audiences are the same arts which give his philosophic poems their conversational tone. And in this technique of addressing the audience one can see the rudiments of dramatic speech. Indeed, many of the philosophic poems are almost monologues, while in others the thesis is developed through the medium of two

6. "Education by Poetry: a Meditative Monologue" (a lecture), *Amherst Graduates' Quarterly, 20* (February, 1931), 84–5. It is possible, though unlikely, that the passage in "Build Soil" was written before the lecture was composed, but in any case the parallel is significant.

speaking characters. Dialogue is natural in poetry of this sort, for a philosophic thesis is a kind of debate with pros and cons. Hence the popularity of the colloquium among philosophers as a means of clarifying difficult ideas. Nothing makes things easier than to have a character who can be depended upon always to ask Socrates the right question. Dialogue is inherent in ideas themselves, and the poet who wishes to explain ideas rather than meditate upon them will naturally be drawn to it. From "The White-Tailed Hornet," where the poet speaks to a general audience, to "The Lesson for Today," in which he speaks to a silent listener (Alcuin), and on to "West-Running Brook," with its fully dramatic dialogue, is an easy transition.

3

The course of Frost's development over the years substantiates this view of his dramatic work. It is a striking fact that when he writes in the pastoral vein he tends to write dramatically. In examining the order in which his poems appeared, we see these two aspects of his art growing up together and so closely connected that one is tempted to consider each a function of the other. Of the twenty dramatic poems I have listed, at least thirteen are pastoral in the full sense of the word, while three others are distinctly regional in setting and subject. Furthermore, among the rest of his poems, the pastorals generally have the strongest dramatic element. The chronology shows that throughout the poet's life his interest in drama has paralleled the evolution of his pastoralism. The table below will help to make this clear. I have listed the dramatic poems in the order of their book publication. In the case of poems written a considerable time before book publication, dates of composition are indicated after the titles.

BOOK	POEM	FORM
A Boy's Will (1913)	none	
North of Boston (1914)	The Death of the Hired Man	dramatic dialogue
	Home Burial	dramatic dialogue
	The Fear	dramatic dialogue
	The Self-Seeker	dramatic dialogue
	The Generations of Men	dramatic dialogue
	A Servant to Servants	dramatic monologue
	The Mountain	pastoral dialogue
	A Hundred Collars	pastoral dialogue
	Blueberries	pastoral dialogue
	The Housekeeper	narrative monologue
Mountain Interval (1916)	In the Home Stretch	dramatic dialogue
	Snow	dramatic dialogue
	The Bonfire	narrative monologue
New Hampshire (1923)	The Witch of Coös	dramatic monologue
	The Pauper Witch of Grafton	dramatic monologue
	A Fountain, a Bottle, a Donkey's Ears, and Some Books	philosophic dialogue
West-Running Brook (1928)	West-Running Brook	philosophic dialogue
A Further Range (1936)	Build Soil (1931-2)	philosophic dialogue
A Witness Tree (1942)	A Literate Farmer and the Planet Venus (1926)	philosophic dialogue
Steeple Bush (1947)	none	
Complete Poems (1949)	From Plane to Plane	philosophic dialogue

Frost's visit to England marks the crucial point in his development as a poet. *A Boy's Will* was published in 1913, shortly after his arrival, but it was mainly written before he left the United States.[7] The poems of this volume are characteristically Edwardian in content and lyric in form. Only a few isolated poems—for example, "Mowing" and "The Tuft of Flowers"—give premonitions of his mature style. A year later he published *North of Boston,* without question his finest single book. *North of Boston* was new in every respect. Here Frost moved from conventional nature poetry to the pastoral eclogue, from the Romantic landscape to the regional scene, from an inherited poetic diction to the language of everyday speech, from a decadent sweetness to an ironic, questioning attitude.

Essentially, *North of Boston* is a book of pastorals. "Mending Wall," "After Apple-Picking," "The Code" are eclogues in the fullest sense. Ten of the sixteen poems in this book are thoroughly pastoral, and all but three are set in New England. It is therefore no small coincidence that *North of Boston* is also pre-eminently a book of dramatic poetry. In fact, it contains the largest quantity of dramatic

7. Concerning the preparation of *A Boy's Will,* see Gorham B. Munson, *Robert Frost: A Study in Sensibility and Good Sense* (New York, 1927), pp. 62–5. Frost sailed for England in September, 1912, and the book was published early in 1913. Considering first the account Munson gives us of Frost's search for a publisher and second the time needed for printing, we may assume that the contents of the volume were determined by December, 1912. In view of this, it seems unlikely that many of the poems in *A Boy's Will* were composed after Frost's arrival in England. That *North of Boston* is almost totally the work of the English sojourn I am firmly convinced, though the information now available to the public is not sufficient to prove the point. The arguments which seem most telling to me are as follows: (1) the poems in *North of Boston* are not only superior to those in the first book, but distinctly different in kind; (2) it seems unlikely that a poet seeking a publisher for his first book would fail to include poems as excellent as most of those in *North of Boston* are, if, at that time, he had already written them. It may be objected that the poems in *North of Boston,* being dramatic and descriptive, were not included in the first book, which is predominately lyric, because they would have seemed out of place. But I question whether there is any strict rationale underlying the selection of poems in *A Boy's Will.* As Munson indicates, Frost seems simply to have culled the best poems he had written by October–November, 1912.

writing to be found in any of Frost's books. Ten poems are cast in the form of dialogue or monologue; exclusive of the masques and the play in verse, a *jeu d'esprit* at best, they make up just half of his dramatic verse. Furthermore, three other poems—"Mending Wall," "The Black Cottage," and "The Code"—show a strong tendency to dramatic speech. Clearly, Frost's dramatic impulse was strongest at the very time when his pastoralism was reaching full development.

Over the years which followed, his dramatic writing evolved with his pastoralism. The next four books, *Mountain Interval, New Hampshire, West-Running Brook,* and *A Further Range,* reveal a gradual shift in his thinking away from the New England subject matter and pastoral form to a more philosophic kind of poetry. As the regional context became less important and he turned from characters and events to ideas, his interest in the dramatic poem declined. He is still the regionalist and pastoralist in *Mountain Interval* and *New Hampshire,* as the titles of these books make plain, and each contains three dramatic poems. But *New Hampshire* marks the end of his main dramatic work; sixteen of the twenty poems had been written by 1923, while another, "A Literate Farmer and the Planet Venus," dates from 1926, though it did not appear until 1942.[8] The title poem of *New Hampshire* shows a synthesis of Frost's pastoralism and his philosophic interests; in *West-Running Brook* the philosophic tendency is dominant.[9] With this decisive turn, the dramatic poem becomes rare. There is only one in *West-Running Brook* and one in *A Further Range* where, as the title announces,

8. That 1926 is the date of composition is indicated beyond reasonable doubt by the mention of this year in the last line of the poem.

9. Concerning the change marked by *West-Running Brook,* an interesting adverse criticism is offered by R. P. Blackmur in a review of *A Further Range,* "The Instincts of a Bard," *The Nation, 142* (1936), 817–9. In my opinion, this is the fairest and most acute treatment of Frost's shortcomings that has yet appeared.

Frost explores areas outside of his regional world. *Steeple Bush* contains none. "From Plane to Plane," which first appeared in *Complete Poems: 1949,* shows that Frost can still write good dramatic verse when he wants to, just as he can still on occasion write a perfect pastoral like "Directive." What the chronology demonstrates is not a decline in dramatic skill, but a shift of interest. The movement away from pastoral toward philosophic poetry meant a movement away from the dramatic.

This is not merely a matter of quantity. A glance at the chronology will show that the relation between pastoral and the dramatic is even more apparent with respect to form. It is in *North of Boston, Mountain Interval,* and *New Hampshire* that we find the most fully dramatic poems, the dialogues and monologues where action is the main interest. After *New Hampshire,* Frost's dramatic poems regularly take the form of what I have called philosophic dialogue. The reader will recall that in this genre the dramatic techniques are subordinated, and the dialogue form serves merely as a means of dramatizing a thesis. "West-Running Brook" occupies a pivotal position in Frost's development. Though it seems to be set in New England, one senses that the sophisticate has replaced the Yankee speaker, and an interest in ideas the methods of pastoral. Its form, the relaxed, conversational dialogue in which events are merely illustrative reflects this change. "Build Soil" and "From Plane to Plane" are of the same type. So too, I believe, are those most unusual poems, *A Masque of Reason* and *A Masque of Mercy.*

No discussion of Frost's dramatic work would be complete without some consideration of the masques. They are poems rich in wit, utterly graceful in the tact with which they treat of the most difficult problems. What other poet could make a success of St. Paul in a Greenwich Village book store or gently parody Yeats' golden bird in "Sailing to Byzantium" while carrying forward an analysis of Job's relation to God? When Job's wife takes a snapshot of her husband, God, and Satan, we realize that only a poet who has mastered every nuance of tone could venture so far as Frost has done in the masques without compromising the seriousness of his subject.

At first the masques may seem to supply abundant evidence of his continuing interest in dramatic poetry. Considering their greater scope, one might even say that they are his most ambitious experiments in the field. They contain, not one or two but as many as five speaking characters, and the usual narrative framework is left out. Yet despite this, the masques are less dramatic in their structure than the poems of *North of Boston,* for in them Frost simply uses on a somewhat larger scale the same form of philosophic dialogue which we have seen in "West-Running Brook."

The characters of the masques are drawn from Old Testament stories. The *Masque of Reason* deals with Job; the *Masque of Mercy* with Jonah. But their stories are not dramatized. Instead we see the characters at a later time. The *Masque of Reason* is a conversation in which Job and his wife ask God why he afflicted Job and are answered, Satan coming in toward the end to add his opinions. In *A Masque of Mercy* Jonah, reincarnate in Jonas Dove, an evangelist, talks over the problem of God's justice with St. Paul and a slightly Bohemian couple who run a book store, Keeper (His Brother's Keeper, the humanist) and Jesse Bel. There is a central action in this masque: Jonas is persuaded to accept St. Paul's idea that God permits injustice in order to overcome justice by mercy; he is further persuaded to go down into the cellar of the book store to contemplate God's mercy, but just as he is about to make the decisive step to the cellar door it slams shut, and he dies of the shock. Jonas cannot commit himself to mercy, because

the only thing he really cares for is justice. The action in
the *Masque of Reason* is more incidental than this. Job's
wife goes to sleep while Job and God argue—women are
not really interested in reason. Satan rides in on a "tendency." Job's wife photographs Job flanked by God and
Satan, showing that the three are aspects of each other and
together make up the human world. In both poems, the
philosophic point is the main thing and the action merely
illustrative, and such excitement as they offer arises from
the rapid interplay of ideas. We do not see the characters
at a moment of crisis, but at a symposium where their ges-
tures, like those of Plato's revelers, merely punctuate the
dispute.

Though Frost in the masques seems to have left north of
Boston, they too, like the philosophic poems, reflect something of his basic pastoral method. Just as the Yankee
speaker reappears in "Build Soil" and "A White-Tailed
Hornet," the masques display the technique of pastoral
contrast. Here, however, it is not a juxtaposing of rural
New England and the outside world. Rather, one sees it
in the ironic difference between the modern setting and
the biblical subject, between the theological problems discussed and the casual idiom in which God, Job, and the
others talk about them. At the beginning of the *Masque of
Reason* God explains:

I've had you on my mind a thousand years
To thank you someday for the way you helped me
Establish once for all the principle
There's no connection man can reason out
Between his just deserts and what he gets.
Virtue may fail and wickedness succeed.
'Twas a great demonstration we put on.

And such a playing of the colloquial tone against the exalted idea is a "great demonstration" of Frost's skill in

adapting the irony of pastoral to the uses of didactic poetry.

The decline of Frost's dramatic writing does not mean a general decline of his powers. The masques, in particular the *Masque of Reason,* are major achievements, and they were written when Frost was over seventy. As we have seen, his interest in drama fades as he turns from regional subjects and the pastoral mode to a poetry of ideas. But the change is not so complete as it may seem, and it would be misleading to suppose that Frost has ever become wholly devoted to philosophizing. Some of his best pastorals— "Desert Places," "Beech," and "Directive" among them— date from the later years. And while "The Lesson for To-day" rather than "Directive" may seem most characteristic of his last books, his writing has never been purely didac- *intended to teach* tic. The speculative concerns of his later verse are balanced by his intense interest in nature. While his unusual gift for nature poetry is not new, it is to this that we are indebted for the majority of Frost's finest poems after *New Hampshire.*

CHAPTER 5

NATURE AND PASTORALISM

Frost has so often written about the rural landscape and wildlife that one can hardly avoid thinking of him as a nature poet. "To the Thawing Wind," "Hyla Brook," "The Oven Bird," "Birches," "A Drumlin Woodchuck"—one could cite such titles by the score. Frost began as a nature poet; "To a Moth Seen in Winter," "Rose Pogonias," "Going for Water" are representative of his work before 1913, and the interest in nature was to persist throughout his career. Frost's nature poetry is so excellent and so characteristic that it must be given a prominent place in any account of his art. In our attempt to understand this aspect of Frost, the idea of pastoral proves useful. Not that the nature poems are to be considered as pastorals in any strict sense—obviously the two kinds of poetry differ. In pastorals the subject is a special society, or, more generally, a way of life, and nature is merely the setting within which we see this. The pastoralist does not write *about* nature; he uses nature as his scene, and it is important only in that it defines the swain's point of view. Nevertheless, Frost's nature poetry is closely related to his pastoralism. One might demonstrate the connection by pointing out how many poems combine both genres. Such pieces as "The Onset," "Unharvested," and "Evening in a Sugar Orchard" present vivid pictures of landscape, but

in them the Yankee point of view through which nature
is seen is as vital to the meaning as the things portrayed.
This is not so in all the nature poems: in a great many
others natural objects hold the center of interest, and the
regional Arcadia with its Yankee characters is absent or
unimportant. The shift in subject is not surprising, for a
poet of rural life would find it natural to write about the
countryside, but the connection between the two poetic
types is more fundamental than this. It consists, I think,
in a similarity of thought, and hence, in a similarity of
poetic design. The basic structure we have noted in his
eclogues appears again as the dominant pattern in the
nature poems. Both kinds of poetry seem to grow from a
single way of looking at reality—the same perspective
which creates pastorals when the poet's eyes are directed
to rural life determines his vision of nature.

That Frost's view of nature is unique may not at first be
apparent, for the modern reader's attitude toward nature
poetry is pretty well determined by the Lake Poets and
their English successors. The very act of writing about
nature seems to mean a commitment to treat it as poets in
England have done since 1800, with the result that most
people take Frost's nature poetry as they take Wordsworth's or Tennyson's. Yet there is a bleakness in his landscape and a sharpness of outline in the imagery quite foreign even to Wordsworth's Cumberland. This cannot be
explained by the difference between localities. "The Oven
Bird" is an entirely different kind of poem from Wordsworth's "To a Skylark," and the dissimilarity has little to
do with the fact that the bird in one poem is American
and in the other English. Another sign of his uniqueness is
that his nature poems do not evoke the same variety of
emotional response. Much of his popularity is traceable to
the fact that he has managed to write of nature without
exploiting the emotional effects which, however fine they

are in Wordsworth and the other Romantics, seem rather shopworn in more recent poets.

Of course no modern nature poet will be able to free himself completely from the Romantic way of treating nature, and in Frost there are many reminiscences of Wordsworth, Keats, and others. But what Frost has derived from tradition is adapted to his own quite different purposes. One may hear the Romantic harmonies in his work, but they reverberate within a world quite changed. When he describes a tree as "Vague dream-head lifted out of the ground,/ And thing next most diffuse to cloud," the Romantic vision is immediately dispelled by the facts of a different landscape—"Not all your light tongues talking aloud/ Could be profound." [1] This is not an ironic rejection of the Romantic attitude; Frost simply does not look at nature through the same eyes. Though critics have pointed out his eminently reasonable view of nature, his farmer's sagacity and unwillingness to go beyond brute facts, they have failed to see the essential difference between his nature poetry and that to which the nineteenth century has conditioned us.

This difference can best be seen by pursuing somewhat further the comparison with Wordsworth. In the poetry of his great period, Wordsworth's theme is the spirit immanent in nature and man. The philosophic ideas through which he seeks to justify this concept of spirit are diverse and combined in a variety of ways, the emphasis shifting from one poem to another. I suspect that Wordsworth's philosophy cannot be systematized, but whether or not this is so, it is not necessary here to untangle the various strands of his thought; for however complex the intellectual background of Wordsworth's Nature may be, his essential poetic idea remains constant—the union of mind and external reality. He expresses this union most often through

1. "Tree at My Window."

suggesting a blending of thought and landscape and portraying the subtle affinities between the natural scene and the moral sentiments. This central theme is reflected in the poetic form. Wordsworth's language has an intended imprecision which suggests both things and thoughts. One sees this in the subdued double entendre of his philosophic terms:

> A motion and a spirit, that impels
> All thinking things, all objects of all thought,
> · And rolls through all things. . . .[2]

The peculiar shift in the meaning of "things" and the way that Newtonian physics and the sublimities of philosophical idealism are blended in terms like "motion," "impels," "rolls" show how far beside the point Empson is in complaining that Wordsworth has muddled his philosophy.[3] The vague suggestiveness of Wordsworth's terms is the medium in which thought and object merge. The same blending is manifested in the kind of vaguely outlined nature imagery Wordsworth and most other Romantics prefer. Their streams, breezes, odors, mists, tangled undergrowth, and twilight have the indistinct quality which allows them to drift into the area of subjective experience.[4] As Wordsworth put it, he prefers the regions "where things are lost in each other, and limits vanish, and aspirations are raised." [5]

A reader accustomed to this kind of nature poetry will find much that is familiar in a poem like "The Wood-

2. "Lines Composed a Few Miles Above Tintern Abbey."

3. *Seven Types of Ambiguity* (London, 1947), pp. 151–4. The view I favor is pretty close to that of F. R. Leavis in "Wordsworth," *Revaluation* (New York, 1947), pp. 154–85.

4. See W. K. Wimsatt, "The Structure of Romantic Nature Imagery," *The Verbal Icon* (Lexington, Kentucky, 1954), pp. 103–16.

5. *The Letters of William and Dorothy Wordsworth: The Late Years*, ed. E. de Selincourt (Oxford University Press, 1939), *1*, 134–5.

Pile." Here Frost's approach to nature seems not unlike Wordsworth's in "Resolution and Independence." True, the manner is more casual; Frost is anecdotal where Wordsworth tends to be didactic. But the poet of "The Wood-Pile" strikes a typically Wordsworthian attitude: he regards his rambles through the countryside as the means of a natural and somewhat mysterious instruction of the soul. There is the same high seriousness and air of ethical purpose. In Frost's poem, as in Wordsworth's, it is tacitly assumed that the poet's stroll will lead to a momentous discovery. And here too, the poet sets out without a plan, unaware of what his goal will be, relying on intuition, waiting for a spontaneous revelation to come to him from nature. The opening lines express an attitude reminiscent of Wordsworth's "wise passiveness":

> Out walking in the frozen swamp one gray day,
> I paused and said, 'I will turn back from here.
> No, I will go farther—and we shall see.'

The true discovery must be fortuitous—he finds the woodpile by the same happy accident that Wordsworth found the leech gatherer. In both poems, there is a sudden recognition, and the significance of the natural scene wells up as if from the subconscious.

But here Frost's similarity to Wordsworth ends. For what he finds at the center of the forest is not an image of the spirit immanent in man and nature, but a symbol of the strictly human spirit and its ability to rise above the physical sphere. The woodpile itself is unimportant. It is meaningful only because it leads to a revelation of human nature:

> I thought that only
> Someone who lived in turning to fresh tasks
> Could so forget his handiwork on which
> He spent himself, the labor of his ax,

> And leave it there far from a useful fireplace
> To warm the frozen swamp as best it could
> With the slow smokeless burning of decay.

The firewood will never be used. The man who cut it can carelessly forget its practical value, because humanity transcends the world of physical need. Man lives "in turning to fresh tasks," in the fulfillment of himself through creativity.

The whole meaning of the poem lies in the difference between nature and man. The cedar swamp is an endless tract without meaning or design:

> The view was all in lines
> Straight up and down of tall slim trees
> Too much alike to mark or name a place by
> So as to say for certain I was here
> Or somewhere else: I was just far from home.

"Far from home"—the search for meaning is really a search for something human within the infinite spaces which Pascal viewed with such horror. The woodpile shows that nature itself cannot provide this human element or give the poet's experience meaning. The only meaning one can find in nature is that imposed upon it by the human mind. The woodpile is the symbol of man's creativity. Its decay does not represent any bond between man and nature. It has been taken into the sphere of human purposes, so that even though abandoned, it has rotted away "To warm the frozen swamp as best it could" like firewood burning on a hearth.

This contrast between man and nature is the central theme of Frost's nature poetry. Whereas Wordsworth sees in nature a mystical kinship with the human mind, Frost views nature as essentially alien. Instead of exploring the margin where emotions and appearances blend, he looks at nature across an impassable gulf. What he sees on the other side is an image of a hard, impersonal reality. Man's physical needs, the dangers facing him, the realities of birth and death, the limits of his ability to know and to act are shown in stark outline by the indifference and inaccessibility of the physical world in which he must live.

Thus Frost sees in nature a symbol of man's relation to the world. Though he writes about a forest or a wildflower, his real subject is humanity. The remoteness of nature reveals the tragedy of man's isolation and his weakness in the face of vast, impersonal forces. But nature also serves to glorify man by showing the superiority of the human consciousness to brute matter. In this respect, nature becomes a means of portraying the heroic. There is a fundamental ambiguity of feeling in Frost's view of nature. It is to be feared as man's cruel taskmaster, scorned as insensible, brutish, unthinking matter; yet it is to be loved, not because it has any secret sympathy for man—"One had to be versed in country things/ Not to believe the phoebes wept" [6]—but rather because it puts man to the test and thus brings out his true greatness:

> When stiff and sore and scarred
> I take away my hand
> From leaning on it hard
> In grass and sand,
>
> The hurt is not enough:
> I long for weight and strength
> To feel the earth as rough
> To all my length. [7]

Such ambiguity indicates the poetic potential of Frost's nature. One sees it in "Birches," where the delicate balance between the desire to withdraw from the world and love

6. "The Need of Being Versed in Country Things."
7. "To Earthward."

of the earth is symbolized in the boy's game of swinging
birch trees; in "The Onset" in the contrast between Frost's
dismay at the descent of winter and his assurance of spring;
in the April day of "Two Tramps in Mud Time," which
gives pleasure and yet is pervaded with the lingering threat
of winter. Though his concept of nature does not allow
for the sublimity one finds in Wordsworth, it has a richness of its own. It is a paradox, and it points toward the
greater paradox in man himself.

Readers who think of Frost as a sketcher of pleasant
landscapes should begin with a poem like "The Most of
It." Here the poet shows us the gulf separating man from
nature in bold outline, and this is probably why the poem
has been generally ignored. The picture he presents is certainly not cheerful, much less pretty. It is impressive. It
demonstrates how exalted an idea of the human mind and
how awesome a view of reality the contrast between man
and nature expresses:

> He thought he kept the universe alone;
> For all the voice in answer he could wake
> Was but the mocking echo of his own
> From some tree-hidden cliff across the lake.
> Some morning from the boulder-broken beach
> He would cry out on life, that what it wants
> Is not its own love back in copy speech,
> But counter-love, original response.
> And nothing ever came of what he cried
> Unless it was the embodiment that crashed
> In the cliff's talus on the other side,
> And then in the far distant water splashed,
> But after a time allowed for it to swim,
> Instead of proving human when it neared
> And someone else additional to him,
> As a great buck it powerfully appeared,

Pushing the crumpled water up ahead,
And landed pouring like a waterfall,
And stumbled through the rocks with horny tread,
And forced the underbrush—and that was all.

There is pathos in this poem but something close to tragedy too. The man's search for a sign of love from nature may be foolish and sentimental to a degree, yet he is wise enough to realize that what he wants is "counter-love, original response" rather than a mere reflection of his own love. It takes a certain toughness to see this, to hold out for the real thing. And the real thing when it comes is so remote from his desires that he cannot recognize it. The magnificent buck which swims toward him from across the lake is "the most of it"—all the nature can give. That this is so shows the completeness of man's isolation, and in this sense the poem is despairing. On the other hand, we see man's true stature in the fact that he cannot ever be satisfied with nature. It merely symbolizes the impersonal force of matter, and his blindness to it is really a measure of his spiritual strength. And as the man in the poem transcends nature through ignorance, the speaker transcends it through knowledge. He recognizes the meaning of the buck; he sees that "that was all" nature could give. He is able to look at the grim reality of nature, to recognize its remoteness and inhumanity, and at the same time to admire its magnificent strength. The vision of the great buck as he "stumbled through the rocks with horny tread,/ And forced the underbrush" reveals not only nature, but the superiority of the human mind which can see it for what it is and no more.

The struggle between the human imagination and the meaningless void man confronts is the subject of poem after poem. Frost develops it in a variety of ways—"Desert Places," "Sand Dunes," and "There Are Roughly Zones" represent different approaches to it. His tone modulates from poem to poem as he moves effortlessly from casual sketches to landscapes of intense agony, but throughout his nature poetry the basic contrast persists. Sometimes it is the subject for witty epigrammatic treatment. "Neither Out Far Nor In Deep," for example, describes people along the shore of a beach staring endlessly out to sea. Their intent gaze is subtly identified with man's half-exploratory, half-defensive watch on the universe:

> They cannot look out far.
> They cannot look in deep.
> But when was that ever a bar
> To any watch they keep?

At other times the contrast is not made explicit but is merely suggested by certain dark undertones. Even in Frost's most cheerful nature sketches there is always a bittersweet quality. Admittedly he can and does enjoy nature. His flowers, trees, and animals are all described with affection, yet none of the nature poems is free from hints of possible danger; under the placid surface there is always the unseen presence of something hostile. "Spring Pools," for example, begins innocently enough with a description of the pools and flowers which one sees in the woodlands in early spring. Then suddenly the tone becomes grave:

> The trees that have it in their pent-up buds
> To darken nature and be summer woods—
> Let them think twice before they use their powers
> To blot out and drink up and sweep away
> These flowery waters and these watery flowers
> From snow that melted only yesterday.

There is something sinister about the way the poem turns out. Spring, traditionally the season of birth, innocence, and joy, ushers in darkness, and the optimistic ending of Shelley's "Ode to the West Wind" is grimly inverted.

Treacherous forces are forever breaking through the pleasant surface of the landscape in this manner. Frost on his nature rambles has the air of someone picking his way through no man's land during an uneasy truce. The weather is bracing, his spirits are high; but he must tread lightly for fear of mines, and there is always the chance that he may stumble upon a bullet-pierced helmet or something worse. At the most unexpected times, he gives glimpses of horror. In "Two Tramps in Mud Time" he interrupts his genial chat about the April weather to advise:

> Be glad of water, but don't forget
> The lurking frost in the earth beneath
> That will steal forth after the sun is set
> And show on the water its crystal teeth.

These vistas opening upon fearful realities do not in the least negate the beauty Frost also sees in nature; rather, it is they which give his songbirds, wild flowers, brooks, and trees their poignant appeal. The charm of many of the nature lyrics results from the vividness with which sweet, delicate things stand out against the somber background. You cannot have the one without the other: love of natural beauty and horror at the remoteness and indifference of the physical world are not opposites but different aspects of the same view.

The difference between a "pretty" nature poem and a poem of sterner vision is merely one of emphasis. For instance, the lyric, "A Boundless Moment," gives us one of those fresh glimpses of beauty which have made Frost's nature poetry so popular, yet it deals with essentially the same view of reality as "Bereft," which is among the poet's saddest and most terrifying poems. The wistfulness of the former lyric is part of its charm:

He halted in the wind, and—what was that
Far in the maples, pale, but not a ghost?
He stood there bringing March against his thought,
And yet too ready to believe the most.

'Oh, that's the Paradise-in-bloom,' I said;
And truly it was fair enough for flowers
Had we but in us to assume in March
Such white luxuriance of May for ours.

We stood a moment so in a strange world,
Myself as one his own pretense deceives;
And then I said the truth (and we moved on).
A young beech clinging to its last year's leaves.

The "boundless moment" gives a vision of beauty, but this vision is merely an illusion—the flowers the two men thought they saw are only dead leaves clinging to a beech. The reader responds to the gorgeous sight of the "paradise-in-bloom," in much the same way as the characters in the poem. But nature itself is barren. When the walkers recognize the leaves for what they are, they can only turn again to the routine of life. The incident shows man's tragic limitations. His imagination cannot sustain the ideal vision long—for a "boundless moment" it can mold nature to its desires, then the "Paradise-in-bloom" again becomes the dead tree of reality. But there is more to the poem than this hard lesson. The fading of a vision may be sad, but the truthfulness which will not take it too seriously has something noble about it. The speaker's refusal to accept anything but the truth, even when the truth is disappointing, demonstrates the courage of man's intellect.

Unflinching honesty in the face of facts is a recurrent theme in Frost's nature poetry. For it is in this that he sees the basis of man's power and indeed of his spiritual being.

Man can never find a home in nature, nor can he live outside of it.[8] But he can assert the reality of his spirit and
thus can exist independently of the physical world in the
act of looking squarely at the facts of nature.

Thus, while "A Boundless Moment" describes a trivial
incident and gives us a pleasant picture with only the
slightest hint of sorrow, it is very much like "Bereft,"
where a scene symbolic of intense sorrow serves to express
the same view of man's relation to nature:

> Where had I heard this wind before
> Change like this to a deeper roar?
> What would it take my standing there for,
> Holding open a restive door,
> Looking down hill to a frothy shore?
> Summer was past and day was past.
> Somber clouds in the west were massed.
> Out in the porch's sagging floor,
> Leaves got up in a coil and hissed,
> Blindly struck at my knee and missed.
> Something sinister in the tone
> Told me my secret must be known:
> Word I was in the house alone
> Somehow must have gotten abroad,
> Word I was in my life alone,
> Word I had no one left but God.

The speaker of this poem has just suffered some terrible
bereavement, and his utter loneliness is embodied in the
bleakness of the landscape. There is something ominous
in the darkening sky and a blind hostility in the dead
leaves which swirl about his legs. He is overwhelmed by
the sense of complete isolation. He has "no one left but
God," and it does not seem that he will find any comfort

8. As the poet once remarked to me, "You know, there is nothing after
this."

there, for God, as he mentions him, is merely the last resort of the desperate. Yet for all its gloom, "Bereft" is not a poem of despair. The very fact that the speaker can recognize in the landscape the full extent of his loneliness shows the mind's capacity for courage.

In both his nature poems and his pastorals the poet portrays average human experience by projecting it into a world remote and distinct. Nature, as Frost conceives it, is really a kind of wild-life Arcadia, and in writing of scenery and animals he uses it in much the same way as he uses the mythic rural New England in his pastorals. Like his rural New England, nature evokes paradoxical attitudes: on the one hand it is a realm of ideals where the essential realities are found in their pristine forms; on the other it is an inferior plane where life is crude, insensate, mechanical. Most important, however, nature is separate, independent, off by itself away from man, just as the country north of Boston is separate from the urban environment of modern America.

And because Frost's basic method is the same, the structure of the nature poems is also similar. As we have already noted, he is able to focus broad areas of experience within his sketches and anecdotes of Yankee life because the very remoteness of the rural scene suggests parallels. The same is true of his nature poetry. By insisting upon the remoteness of nature he directs attention to the patterns in nature which correspond to those in human experience. In "Nothing Gold Can Stay" this analogical method is obvious:

> Nature's first green is gold,
> Her hardest hue to hold.
> Her early leaf's a flower;
> But only so an hour.
> Then leaf subsides to leaf.

So Eden sank to grief,
So dawn goes down to day.
Nothing gold can stay.

The first five lines are mainly descriptive, and it may seem that the poem merely expresses regret for the transience of natural beauty. Then, in the sixth line, the image is suddenly placed in a new context. The loss of beauty in the leaf is likened to the loss of innocence in Eden. One feels a mixture of sadness and inevitability in the change from gold to green. The subject is not just the passing of a beautiful sight, but the corruption which seems to be a necessary part of maturing. The fall of man reveals this in human nature taken as a whole, and through the next image—"So dawn goes down to day"—we see the same process in the cosmos. Since the period from dawn to sunset is the established symbol of the individual life span, one can hardly avoid the suggestion that each man suffers a similar loss as he develops from childhood to maturity. However, this need not be insisted upon; what is important is Frost's method of comparing a process in the human sphere with a process in nature. The analogies do not weaken his description—quite the opposite. The leaves seem preternaturally bright, because they hold so much meaning for man. We do not look away from the leaves to Eden, to dawn, to the life of the average man. We see all in a single line of vision. This is the perspective of pastoral, and when we turn from imagery to the emotional tone of the poem, we find a characteristically pastoral irony. The tiny leaves, seemingly so trivial, enfold the problem of man's fate!

Frost does not always spell out his parallels in such an explicit way. As a rule the analogies are implied rather than stated. By insisting on the remoteness of nature he can suggest ever-widening circles of correspondences in the

human sphere without seeming to depart from pure description. "Range-Finding" is a good illustration of the
way this is done:

> The battle rent a cobweb diamond-strung
> And cut a flower beside a ground bird's nest
> Before it stained a single human breast.
> The stricken flower bent double and so hung.
> And still the bird revisited her young.
> A butterfly its fall had dispossessed
> A moment sought in air his flower of rest,
> Then lightly stooped to it and fluttering clung.
> On the bare upland pasture there had spread
> O'ernight 'twixt mullein stalks a wheel of thread
> And straining cables wet with silver dew.
> A sudden passing bullet shook it dry.
> The indwelling spider ran to greet the fly,
> But finding nothing, sullenly withdrew.

The upland pasture contains two distinct worlds, the bat-
tlefield where the human struggle is played out and the
realm of the bird, the butterfly, and the spider. Though
man's world is superimposed upon theirs, he cannot ever
penetrate it. A flower is bent double by a range-finding
bullet, but the creatures of the field go about their life
undisturbed. And even should the battle burn out the
grass and destroy its inhabitants, man will not truly have
broken in upon this other world, for the issues of victory,
courage, and suffering can have no meaning in nature.

What the contrast reveals is something far more subtle
than mere difference. The world of nature comes to serve
as a commentary on the human world, as we see in the
way the spider responds to the range-finding bullet. The
bullet has been fired with the sinister intent of groping out
a human target, but for him it is only a false alarm and he

"sullenly" withdraws. Granted that human concerns are nothing to him, yet his nonchalance at a moment when men are about to be slaughtered by the thousands is startling. But in a sense he is right. It matters little to him what shook his web, so long as it was not a fly. If he is ignorant of what the bullet portends for him, perhaps it is for the best, for though the tanks are about to grind over him there is no way to escape. In terms of his own world, the spider is perfectly wise. The slightest vibration sends him scurrying up his cables—how much more subtle than the brute force of the bullet, which only approximates its target! One admires the delicate response of the spider because, in his closed world, he is perfectly efficient, and so too are the ground bird as she hovers tenderly over her young and the butterfly delicately poised on the broken flower.

This view of nature has the same fundamental irony one finds in Frost's pastoral scenes. It suggests that the natural world is better than man's. It is pure, simple, innocent. Man's cruel purposes cannot invade it. At the same time, however, we are not allowed to forget that it is far below the human sphere. The spider, the ground bird, and the butterfly are ignorant of the bullet's momentous meaning. They live mechanically and are incapable of the intense suffering of the human struggle.

But Frost does more here than give us a picture of nature. The poem is about the beginning of a battle. The irony the comparison with nature reveals serves as a means of evaluating this battle, and by extension all warfare. Human acts are decisive. While nature goes on blindly in an unchanging pattern and with a power undiminished, the range-finder will eventually feel out his target, and men will die. For man death is an absolute, and this makes the events of his life meaningful. The passing bullet is not just an accident. It symbolizes the very issue of survival.

Man's consciousness of death shows how wide the human range of experience is compared with nature's narrow confines. He thinks, he feels, he suffers, while nature only exists. Granted, the battle represents folly and cruelty, but it also represents man's intense awareness of life. This awareness is only possible on the human plane, where consciousness gives the individual a life separate from that of the species and thus makes real death possible. Nature, which cannot die, though the particular spider and bird may be killed, does not really live either. And by the same token, only the human act has ethical meaning. The spider is a mere predator; the bird's care for her young is just instinct. Only man is capable of the bullet's malice. Only in the human battle are cruelty and heroism possible.

I have discussed the nature poems in which suffering is the subject because in them we see most clearly how the contrast between man and nature enables Frost to deal with major issues of human life. But the contrast reveals beauty as well as horror, love as well as loneliness. Frost's affection for nature, like his fear of it, is based on a sense of analogy. "Two Look at Two" is a perfect example. A young couple out for an evening walk have climbed part way up a wooded hillside, when darkness comes and they can go no further. They feel a wistful disappointment. It would be nice to go on, to penetrate deeper into nature, but it is too dark and the "failing path" would be treacherous:

> They stood facing this,
> Spending what onward impulse they still had
> In one last look the way they must not go . . .
>   'This is all,' they sighed,
> 'Goodnight to woods.' But not so; there was more.

A doe and after her "an antlered buck of lusty nostril" appear on the other side of the wall to stare at them in

blank puzzlement and then pass on unscared. To the deer
they appear as mysterious as the deer seem to them:

> Two had seen two, whichever side you spoke from.
> 'This *must* be all.' It was all. Still they stood,
> A great wave from it going over them,
> As if the earth in one unlooked-for favor
> Had made them certain earth returned their love.

It is the very distance between humanity and nature that
makes the recognition so poignant. The man and woman
cannot enter nature or identify themselves with it. Symbolically, they must stop at a wall—beyond this the path is
too dangerous. They do not dare "To stretch a proffering
hand—and a spell-breaking." The deer would merely run
away. They can only reach nature in thought through the
recognition of analogy. The words " 'This *must* be all.'
It was all" echo the grim conclusion of "The Most of It"
—"and that was all." There the great buck represented
the remoteness of nature; in this poem the deer are a sign
of something parallel in nature and man. But there is still
the impassable gulf—the horror at man's isolation and the
delight in finding resemblances are aspects of a single view.

Wherever Frost treats nature sympathetically, one finds
this process of discovering analogies. Whether he writes
about a songbird or a seascape there is always a glimpse of
something ironically parallel to human experience. The
sweet pathos of "The Oven Bird" comes from the tone of
human regret in his song. He sings sadly of summer, re-
membering spring, just as man looks upon his everyday
life with the discontent of one who judges reality by the
dream of Eden:

> The question that he frames in all but words
> Is what to make of a diminished thing.

In "Devotion" the shore holds the sea in a lover's embrace:

> The heart can think of no devotion
> Greater than being shore to ocean—
> Holding the curve of one position,
> Counting an endless repetition.

"Hyla Brook," "Unharvested," "Canis Major," "The Last Mowing," and "Tree at My Window" represent variations of the same basic pattern. And comparing these more cheerful pieces with such poems as "Design" and "Desert Places," one sees that the analogical design can, by a slight shift of emphasis, reveal the horror rather than the beauty in nature.

A final aspect of the nature poetry and one of the most important is Frost's strong tendency to personification. The device is common enough in poems about nature, and most readers are likely to take an unfavorable view of it. It suggests a sentimental pantheism or oversimple allegorizing. Frost's personifications, however, are different from those to which the Romantics have accustomed us. Their personifications generally take the form of brief metaphor, while his are nearly always extended analogies. Keats' ode, "To Autumn," illustrates the point well, for while the season is likened to a woman, the poet does not develop the comparison, but rather suggests through a series of brilliant descriptive images her mysterious presence in the autumn scene. The human and the natural are not compared but blended. Obviously Frost's mode of personification is more explicit and consciously rendered. He does not merely liken things in nature to man, he explores the resemblance, usually at some length. Analogy is the lens through which he examines nature, and personification, which is simply the analogy between man and a natural object, is therefore a primary means of seeing. Frost's preference for personification is indicative of his whole manner of conceiving nature, for such a mode of sustained comparison is only possible within the framework of a world view in which the natural and the human are conceived as distinct and separate yet parallel planes.

This contrast makes the human qualities of Frost's animals stand out with startling boldness. The effect is a quaintness and extravagance which seem more akin to the medieval beast fable than to Romantic nature poetry. Often his personifications approach the absurd, as in "The Runaway," where the folksy and almost lugubrious tone illustrates how easily the device may get out of hand. Frost seems to be aware of the danger, however, for generally his treatment of animals is humorous. Consider the fine irony of the epigram entitled "Waspish":

> On glossy wires artistically bent,
> He draws himself up to his full extent.
> His natty wings with self-assurance perk.
> His stinging quarters menacingly work.
> Poor egotist, he has no way of knowing
> But he's as good as anybody going.

While such humor may be a necessary safeguard against absurdity, Frost's technique of personification serves serious purposes, and it would be an error to mistake his animal poems for mere light verse. "Departmental," for example, may be taken as a comic poem, but its humor is actually a means of portraying such serious matters as the blinding effects of custom and the indifference of the group to the individual. The poem is a perfect illustration of his pastoral method. Here human society is viewed through the analogy of an ant hive, and we are made to see the absurdity of man's allegiance to an impersonal social order by watching the ants as they discover the death of one of their workers:

> Ants are a curious race;
> One crossing with hurried tread

> The body of one of their dead
> Isn't given a moment's arrest—
> Seems not even impressed.
> But he no doubt reports to any
> With whom he crosses antennae,
> And they no doubt report
> To the higher up at court.
> Then word goes forth in Formic:
> 'Death's come to Jerry McCormic.'

The poem then describes with savage irony the governmental red tape of the instructions for Jerry's burial, the mortician-ant's cold professionalism, and the general indifference of the public. By picturing the ant colony as a miniature society, Frost reveals the resemblance between the stultifying effects of departmentalism among men and the blindly mechanical operations of insect life. The whimsical effects of the comparison are of the very essence, for the poem is funny just because it explores the resemblance between ants and men so thoroughly. And such thoroughness is only possible for a poet who sees man and nature separated by a boundary which is both definite and inalterable.

CHAPTER 6

FROST AS MODERN POET

The present chapter is frankly speculative. My intent is to offer a few remarks on the development of Frost's art and its relation to poetry in the twentieth century. The effort to define a poet's thought is apt to be a perilous enterprise, but in the case of Frost the attempt needs to be made, for many of the misunderstandings about his poems result from the difficulty of locating his place in contemporary literature. One objective of this chapter will therefore be to point out his modernity; and this subsumes the other, which is to define some of the problems with which his poetry deals.

Such an exploration may best begin with the similarity we have noted between the nature poems and the pastorals. The duality of vision they manifest is a dominant characteristic of Frost's thought, and its origin can be most clearly discerned in his concept of nature. For Frost, nature is really an image of the whole world of circumstances within which man finds himself. It represents what one might call "the human situation." "Bereft" and "Once by the Pacific" illustrate the point well, but it is clearest in "The Star-Splitter," where the hero is led by his discouragement at the difficulties of his work to buy a telescope so that he may contemplate the stars which had seemed to ridicule his "hugger-mugger farming." The relationship between man and nature represents the whole problem raised by the opposition of mind and matter, of man's actual experience with its feelings, purposes, and intuitions of value and a scientific scheme of reality in which everything is reducible to matter and process. Frost's persistent concern with the remoteness of nature manifests his desire to accept the scientific scheme. Such acceptance would seem to be dictated by common sense— as Falstaff says, "Is not the truth the truth?" But poetry is concerned with the very elements of experience which the scientific scheme excludes, and the poet who wishes to be loyal to scientific truth is faced with a difficult problem. If the "real" world is the world as science describes it, are feelings, purposes, and values "unreal"? Or is the actual lived experience in which they are infused a mere illusion? The unique form of Frost's nature poetry represents his way of resolving the problem, and it is, I suggest, an essentially modern solution.

A passage from Whitehead's *Science and the Modern World* will prove relevant. In surveying the history of science, Whitehead contends that beginning with the scientists of the Renaissance there developed a scheme of reality which has dominated Western thought to the present century:

> There persists . . . throughout the whole period the fixed scientific cosmology which presupposes the ultimate fact of an irreducible brute matter, or material, spread throughout space in a flux of configurations. In itself such a material is senseless, valueless, purposeless. It just does what it does do, following a fixed routine imposed by external relations which do not spring from the nature of its being.[1]

This sums up rather well the tacit assumptions underlying such a poem as "The Most of It," and Whitehead's his-

1. New York, Mentor Books, 1958, p. 18.

torical perspective makes it clear that the problem at the center of Frost's nature poems is hardly new. He explains that while from the beginning there were continual attempts to modify this scheme of reality, such efforts could not succeed, because even those most opposed to it shared the tacit assumptions upon which the system rested. They were, so to speak, imprisoned by the concepts of science. So long as one assumes the irreducible brute matter Whitehead describes in the passage I have quoted, so long as one assumes the kind of space and the kind of time it postulates, one cannot break out of the Newtonian universe. Whitehead's purpose, of course, is to show how the new physics which began with Einstein alters basic concepts so as to make possible a more satisfactory world view. But such revision could hardly have affected Frost's basic conception of nature, which had already taken its characteristic form by 1914, five years before the general relativity theory was confirmed by experiment and a good many more before people other than specialists could begin to grasp what the discoveries meant.

The problem which science posed for Frost and the other poets who came to maturity in the period 1910–20 was the same as that which had confronted the Romantics and Victorians. How was the poet to portray human experience with its sensations, its emotions, its knowledge of good and evil, indeed, its very awareness of consciousness itself and yet at the same time recognize the validity of the scientific scheme, where everything is reduced to "the hurrying of material, endlessly, meaninglessly?" [2] For Frost's generation the question was harder and more urgent because by the turn of the century many of the more likely answers had been tried and proved inadequate. But the question had been there for a very long time—even in Pope, who appears to embrace science with

2. ibid., p. 56.

a good deal of enthusiasm, there is a conflict between natural law and the hierarchy of values. The God of "An Essay on Man" may be wise in refusing to alter the fixed laws of nature for any human considerations, but Pope's witty effects develop largely from the sense that physics contradicts other aspects of the divine plan. "And now a bubble burst, and now a world" has more than a little shock value.

After this, the antiscientific bias of the Romantics is hardly surprising. The philosophic background of Romantic nature is far too complex a matter to be considered here, but the general intent of the Romantics is clear. They sought to solve the problem by asserting the unity of man and nature. Whether this involved seeing man as a part of nature, intuiting the common spirit infused in both, or seeing both as parts of a larger reality, the result was a humanizing of nature and a stressing of the emotional values in the landscape. In the course of the nineteenth century, this solution came to seem less and less adequate. Not that the Victorian poets merely copied the Romantics in their treatment of nature. Their nature poetry has its own distinctive qualities, but it is, I think, founded upon Romantic premises. It is possible that a poetic mode had simply worn out, but more likely, the gradual loss of faith in Romantic nature was caused by the increasing authority of science and its intrusion into new areas. In Wordsworth and Coleridge the portrayal of nature is combined with a good deal of philosophic speculation, which interprets and justifies it, but in the Victorians this intellectual framework is absent. Tennyson's argument in *In Memoriam* is not related to the *technique* of nature description he uses, whereas Wordsworth's argument in *The Prelude* is concerned with the very things which the descriptive technique demonstrates. Arnold often finds himself in the position of openly rejecting the premises from which his methods of describing nature are derived! One cannot help feeling that by mid-century the progress of science had swept away the intellectual foundations of Romantic nature poetry. I do not mean that it had refuted the abstract theories the Romantics favored —Hartleyan psychology, philosophical idealism, Neoplatonism, and the rest—but that it had killed their fundamental belief in nature as a divine creation embodying the spiritual and moral law. When Tennyson speaks of "Nature, red in tooth and claw" (*In Memoriam* LVI), we see how much, since the beginning of the century, the concept of nature had been narrowed to fit the scientific scheme. The Romantics would never have had such a thought; they did not confront a nature so emptied of moral and spiritual content. By the end of the nineteenth century the Romantic vision of nature had ceased to seem valid as a way of reconciling scientific fact with the perceptions of the imagination.

Modern poetry may be said to have begun as a fresh attempt to solve the problem posed by science. Imagism, for example, represents an attempt to confront the physical facts of reality in the most direct way. The Imagists tended to advocate an abandonment of overtly stated ideas and sentiments, because these stand between the poet and the actual things of his experience. Yet for the Imagists the proper content of poetry was not really things described but the sensations of perceiving them, and so, in an important way, Imagism represents a retreat. It limits poetry to the narrow range of sense impressions and thus concedes that the autonomous material being with which science deals is outside the poet's range. Indeed, it is not hard to see in Imagism the same division between poetry and science which had been proposed by Bacon and Hobbes—that between sense experience, which is subjective, and the realm of actual being, which is comprehended by reason. The Imagist distrust of ideas in poetry is indicative. It was to be Symbolism rather than Imagism which would provide the more satisfactory answer, and the Symbolist verse of Pound, Eliot, and Yeats represents the dominant mode of modern poetry, one which seems even more characteristic of the age in that its basic techniques are reflected in the major contemporary novelists. The apparent difference between Frost's verse and Symbolist poetry makes his work seem out of place in contemporary literature. Yet if "modern" is a meaningful term, it is neither fair nor accurate to deny his modernity. He is not only a poet of the twentieth century, but one who, in his own way, deals with the very problem which is the concern of the Symbolists.

The connection between his art and the more characteristic modern poetry can best be seen by noting their structural resemblance. Both Frost and the Symbolists tend to view reality through the perspective of contrasting levels of being. In Frost's nature poems this technique quite obviously results from his desire to recognize the validity of science. Thus, despite his indebtedness to Romanticism, he must be seen as essentially anti-Romantic. By insisting on the gulf separating man and nature, he directly opposes the Romantic attempt to bring the two together. While the Romantics sought a place for sensations, feelings, and values within physical nature, he conceives of the physical world as a distinct level of being. And just because of this, he is able to avoid the assumption that the physical world comprises the whole of reality. He can accept nature as the limited, purely physical world which science depicts and yet place it within a larger context which includes the realities of purpose, feeling, and value. His method is to unify scientific nature and the realm of human experience, not by blending them, but by viewing reality as a vista of distinct but parallel planes.

In Symbolism one finds much the same kind of perspective, though it is developed in a different way. While there is great diversity between symbolist poets, they do, I think, share certain common tendencies. Their use of a deep historical vista and their characteristic interest in archaeology, anthropology, and philology indicate their intent to find for intuitions of value a firm basis in scientific fact. The imaginative logic of Symbolism would seem to go as follows: Symbols are an historical reality, that is, we know them as actual works of art, and every society, past or present, has produced symbolic representations of some sort. Further, a symbol has meaning, it was made to express this meaning, and though meaning is concerned with mental and spiritual things outside of the scientific scheme, one can believe that it too is real, for the symbol which expresses it is real. It follows that the things the meaning reveals are also real in that they have had the power to create the symbol. The symbol transcends time. While it was made in a particular time, its meaning continues to reside in it and is available to men living many centuries thereafter. Furthermore, symbols indicate a universal pattern in experience, for anthropology tends to show that in the art of many diverse societies there are certain common symbolic patterns. The symbol, then, provides a basis for accepting the realities which science does not account for, not only through the meaning it expresses, but by the very fact that it does express meaning—its very existence tends to prove the truth of the things it represents. Admittedly, the logic of this reasoning is not impeccable, but it has sufficed to give the subjective aspects of symbolist poetry some of the authority of scientific fact.

It is quite natural that Symbolist poetry should involve both a very strong historical orientation and a critique of the concept of time. Poetry of this kind requires that the symbol be seen in its various manifestations, and this means a constant reference backward from the present to

other periods more or less remote. Thus Symbolism creates a very acute awareness of the distance between the past
and the present, and of the passing of time. But, paradoxi-
cally, it also leads to a denial of time and an historical
sense which, in Eliot's words, "involves a perception, not
only of the pastness of the past, but of its presence." [3] For
the work of art, as we have seen, transcends time, and the
emergence of the same symbolic forms in the art of epochs
remote from one another represents the similarity of these
epochs and the unchanging aspects of experience. Whitehead has pointed out that a linear conception of time is
essential to pre-relativity science.[4] The historical consciousness of the Symbolist poets, like Frost's insistence
on the remoteness of nature, indicates an acceptance of the
prevailing scientific scheme, but such an acceptance is
only possible when the lineal scheme is combined with
its opposite, the concept of eternity. Yeats' cyclical theory
of history and Eliot's analysis of time in "Burnt Norton"
illustrate this well.

In "The Waste Land," one can see how directly the dual
conception of time leads to that technique of contrasting
disparate contexts so characteristic of Symbolist poetry.
Cleanth Brooks, in his well-known analysis of this poem,
summarizes Eliot's method of poetic organization as follows:

> The basic method used in "The Waste Land" may
> be described as the application of the principle of com-
> plexity. The poet works in terms of surface paral-
> lelisms which in reality make ironical contrasts, and
> in terms of surface contrasts which in reality consti-
> tute parallelisms. (The second group sets up effects
> which may be described as the obverse of irony.) The
> two aspects taken together give the effect of chaotic

3. "Tradition and the Individual Talent," *Selected Essays, 1917–1932*
(New York, Harcourt, Brace, 1932), p. 4.
4. Whitehead, pp. 118–30.

experience ordered into a new whole, though the realistic surface of experience is faithfully retained. . . .

The fortune-telling of "The Burial of the Dead" will
illustrate the general method very satisfactorily. On
the surface of the poem the poet reproduces the pat-
ter of the charlatan, Madam Sosostris, and there is
the surface irony: the contrast between the original
use of the Tarot cards and the use made by Madame
Sosostris. But each of the details (justified realistically
in the palaver of the fortune-teller) assumes a new
meaning in the general context of the poem. There is
then, in addition to the surface irony, something of a
Sophoclean irony too, and the "fortune-telling," which
is taken ironically by a twentieth-century audience,
becomes *true* as the poem develops—true in a sense
in which Madame Sosostris herself does not think it
true. . . . The items of her speech have only one
reference in terms of the context of her speech: the
"man with three staves," the "one-eyed merchant,"
the "crowds of people walking round in a ring," etc.
But transferred to other contexts they become loaded
with special meanings.[5]

Though Brooks is primarily concerned with the irony
emanating from Eliot's symbols, his statement provides a
valuable definition of the structure beneath this irony.
Eliot's technique, as he points out, is that of movement
from one context to another. In this way the poet reveals
the full meaning of his symbols and brings out the underlying resemblances between the diverse persons, episodes,
and objects, with the result that these disparate materials
are united within a single vision. For instance, the symbols
of the Tarot cards reappear on several different levels: in

5. *Modern Poetry and The Tradition* (Chapel Hill, University of North
Carolina Press, 1939), p. 167.

the literary context of Shakespeare's *The Tempest,* in the historical context of the fertility rites reported by Frazer, in the myth of the Fisher King, and in the scenes of the modern metropolis. It is obvious, then, that Eliot's method depends upon his exploring a series of discrete contexts.

In this we see a fundamental similarity to Frost's pastoral perspective. Both poets assume a world composed of isolated levels of being, and thus both tend to see experience and portray it as a totality of sharply differing contexts. Where Frost juxtaposes rural and urban life, the regional and the cosmopolitan, the human and the natural, Eliot contrasts the social classes and holds up disparate historical periods for comparison. In both, too, the contrasting planes are not only different but parallel. They are held together and made to interpret each other by a dominant sense of analogy. Thus in "The Waste Land" one finds ranges of correspondence similar to those evoked by Frost's symbols. The wealthy neurotic at her dressing table is reflected both in Philomela and the woman being discussed by her vulgar friend in a pub; Elizabeth, Cleopatra, a stenographer of easy virtue, and the Rhine maidens are ranged in a single perspective; biblical scenes parallel pagan myths; arias from Wagner blend with echoes from the *Divine Comedy.* Eliot is not simply balancing off disparate items. Each introduces its entire context, and, at the same time, each reflects within its context some element of the myth, which, as a key analogy, joins all the contexts together. Similarly, in Frost's poetry the regional world is kept quite separate from the everyday life of urban society, and nature from the level of human experience; yet the separate contexts, though never allowed to merge, are held together by the contrast between them, which creates a constant reference from one to the other and an awareness of ironic parallels.

In comparing the poetry of Frost and Eliot, I do not

for a moment mean to suggest that their work is really quite similar. Obviously any such claim would be absurd. The comparison is of value, however, in that it shows a structural element which is fundamental to both and which in both seems to have developed as a means of coping with the problem posed by science. By noting this similarity we can see more clearly Frost's place in modern literature. It demonstrates that he is an intellectual as well as a chronological contemporary of the Symbolist poets and that his pastoral mode, while leading to a kind of poetry quite different from that of Symbolism, belongs in the same chapter of literary history.

So far I have discussed mainly the pastoral structure as it appears in the nature poems, since here the origins of this structure seem most apparent. But the link between the nature poems and the true pastorals is a strong one, and the typically modern concerns and methods which we have noted in Frost's treatment of nature tell us much about the origins of the pastorals themselves. The important connection between these two kinds of poetry becomes apparent when one observes their parallel development.

It is a significant fact that Frost wrote nature poems which display the kind of pastoral design we have been considering many years before he produced pastorals. "To a Moth Seen in Winter," which the poet dates "circa 1900," shows that even at that early date his characteristic conception of nature had already formed. In this poem he describes the futility of the moth which has emerged from its chrysalis in wintertime to seek a mate it will never find. As the moth rests momentarily on his hand, he muses:

> You must be made more simply wise than I
> To know the hand I stretch impulsively
> Across the gulf of well nigh everything
> May reach to you, but cannot touch your fate.

Then in the concluding lines, which follow directly, he draws an analogy between the moth's little tragedy and his own human fate:

> I cannot touch your life, much less can save,
> Who am tasked to save my own a little while.

Not only do these lines epitomize the view of nature characteristic of his mature verse, but, what is even more significant, they show that from a very early date the idea of nature's remoteness is bound up with the habit of seeing reality in terms of contrasting planes. It is in passages like these that Frost's mature art first begins to emerge.

The pastoralism of the New England poems represents Frost's most fully realized development of the way of thinking implicit in such early nature sketches. When *North of Boston* is compared with *A Boy's Will*, it becomes apparent that the poet found his true medium when he discovered New England. The earlier volume gives glimpses of what is to come, but it is not until his second book that he begins to portray regional life in earnest, and it is just at this point that he first shows complete mastery of the pastoral form. The sudden maturing of his pastoralism in *North of Boston* is paralleled by a simultaneous maturing of his treatment of nature. Frost has called *North of Boston* a "book of people," and it is largely devoted to pictures of regional life in which dramatic action and character analysis are the dominant interests. However, it does contain one nature poem, "The Wood-Pile," which is superior to any he had hitherto written. "The Wood-Pile" marks a distinct turning. The nature poems written after it are clearly superior to those which came before. Compare "Ghost House," "My November Guest," or "A Line-Storm Song" with "Hyla Brook," "The Oven Bird," or "The Onset": the latter have a new vigor, a tautness in the line of reasoning, a greater refinement of perception in the imagery. Of course, not all the later nature poems display this new vigor, nor do all the early ones lack merit. The point is that Frost did not write great nature poems until he learned to write great eclogues. One may find an occasional poem like "Misgiving" after *North of Boston,* but one will not find a poem like "The Wood-Pile" before.

In tracing this parallel development I do not mean to imply that Frost's pastoralism grew out of his nature poetry—certainly not that he gave up nature poetry when he had fully developed his pastoral method. He has written nature poems throughout his career, and indeed in his later years more poems of this type have come from his pen than pastorals. His simultaneous growth in these two kinds of poetry, like the similarity of their structural design, indicates that both grew up in response to the same intellectual stimulus. We have seen that his special way of depicting nature is a means of dealing with the problem which science posed for the modern poet. It therefore appears that his pastoralism provides a means of dealing with a similar problem. It is that of preserving within the disorganized world created by science the sense of order and unity a meaningful life requires. In his pastorals, Frost's dominant motive is to reassert the value of individual perception against the fragmenting of experience resulting from modern technology. They thus deal with one of the most fundamental concerns of twentieth–century thought. It is an issue which has had no small effect on Eliot's and Pound's efforts to develop a concept of culture. One sees it too as a motive in Yeats' thought. It is the central theme of countless modern works of social criticism.

It is true that Frost's solution to this problem involves a withdrawal from the modern city to an agrarian world which belongs to the past. He has, in effect, found a retreat in one of those out-of-the-way places where technology has not yet complicated life by separating man from the land.

But this retreat is of a special sort. He does not turn his back on the world of today, nor does he advocate a "return to the soil." There is in his regionalism no call for action or program for social reform, and as a matter of fact he insists over and over again that no program will ever resolve the basic conflicts in human life.[6] His withdrawal must be distinguished from agrarianism. It is the adopting of an artistic perspective. Regional New England—just because it is primitive and remote from modern life—is for him a medium for examining the complex urban world of today, a standard by which to evaluate it, and a context within which to discover the order underlying experience that modern life has obscured and confused.

This point deserves a good deal of emphasis, for there is a tendency, even among the poet's warmest admirers, to view his preoccupation with rural New England as merely an escape from problems too overwhelming to be faced. Those who judge him in this way fail to see the positive value of his retreat for the intellect. Indeed, one may say they have failed really to read him at all.

Granted that Frost's approach is indirect. His evaluation of the everyday urban world is implied rather than stated. Yet is not such indirection in the nature of all poetry? At its best poetry is always oblique, because it is properly concerned with issues so difficult that they will not yield to the frontal assaults of logical argumentation. The fundamental problems with which poets concern themselves are not limited to those they can state in simple, direct terms —one can see this as clearly in Milton, Pope, or Wordsworth as in Eliot. The indirection of poetry is perhaps most obvious in pastoral, since this genre has always been

6. For those interested in Frost's social views, "Build Soil" and the preface which Frost wrote to Edwin Arlington Robinson's *King Jasper* (New York, 1935), pp. v–xv, are among the most important of his writings.

one which deals with major issues in a minor key. If Frost's regional poems are at fault because they are remote from the main problems of their time, then the great pastorals of the Renaissance can be condemned on the same ground. To appreciate Frost's modernity, we must have some knowledge of the special advantages which the pastoral vision offers. We must recognize that in some respects the retreat to a remote rural world can provide the most trenchant analysis and the most subtle evaluation of the world the poet seems to be escaping from.

The nature of Frost's pastoral retreat can best be seen by observing the difference between his poetry and that of the Georgians. The comparison is instructive, for it was with certain members of this group that Frost was closely associated during those crucial months in England when he wrote the greater portion of *North of Boston*. The Georgians too were interested in a poetry of rural life and sought, like him, to bring the language of everyday speech into their verse. Their influence upon his development must have been of the most beneficial kind. Doubtless it was the encouragement of such men as Lascelles Abercrombie and Wilfred Gibson which gave him the confidence needed to discover that the rural life he knew was his real subject and his own way of speaking, with its Yankee qualities of understatement and playful irony, his proper medium. Yet for all this, there is a vital difference between the man from New Hampshire and his English friends. The Georgians, like other poets, were half-consciously groping toward a solution to the problem posed by scientific thought. At its best, their poetry represents an attempt to discover human values in the hard, realistic fact, but they had no very clear notion of the problem they faced and hence no definite program. It is inaccurate to think of them as a coherent group advocating a particular kind of poetry.[7] What they shared was a common sensibility, one which recoiled from the drab sameness of urban life and sought to find in the countryside the color, romance, and rude spontaneity which industrialism had banished from the life of the average Englishman.

There was a basic confusion in the thought of the Georgians, or, to put the matter less kindly, a failure to think. One gets the impression that they reacted mainly against the ugliness of industrialism and failed to see that it was not the mere lack of color that starved the imagination, but the fragmenting of experience caused directly and indirectly by science. They assumed that if the poet could search out those isolated areas as yet unblighted by the factory system he would also find a genuine poetry. They espoused a mild exoticism, turning from the everyday scene to the countryside they had known in boyhood or to the farm village and heath of their weekend rambles. Here, it seemed, they could avoid sentimentality, for in such settings there was an intrinsic charm in the matters of fact they reported. But out-of-the-way places are of little interest unless they are shown within a larger view of reality, and such a larger view the Georgians failed to create. As Samuel Chew rather harshly comments, "The 'Georgians' did not extend the boundaries of poetry, and it is obvious today that theirs was not a revolution but a retreat." [8]

Although it was under Georgian influence that Frost first began to write of regional life, the sentimental rusticity of their verse is quite unlike his vision of New England. The Georgians do no more than paint the rural scene; Frost discovered how to shape it into a mythic world

7. See Frank Swinnerton, *The Georgian Scene: A Literary Panorama* (New York, 1934), pp. 272–7.

8. "Poetry in the Twentieth Century," in *A Literary History of England*, ed. Albert C. Baugh (New York, Appleton Century, 1948), p. 1579.

within which he could express symbolically other ranges of experience. The Georgians retreat to the country is *only* an escape; Frost's is a fresh approach to reality.

We can see the positive nature of this approach by noting the forthright way in which he proclaims his desire to withdraw. He has adopted this as a major theme in his poetry, and he never justifies it on the grounds that urban life is uncomfortable or ugly. Rather, he makes it plain that the world he has escaped to is harder and more demanding. As "After Apple-Picking," "Two Tramps in Mud-Time," and a great many other poems show, one of the central elements in the appeal which back-country New England has for him is that there the life of the imagination can be made to coincide with the humble business of earning a living, in the same way that one's "two eyes make one in sight." The often-quoted line from his early poem, "Mowing"—"The fact is the sweetest dream that labor knows"—strikes the tonic note of all his regional verse. Obviously, there is much in the theme of retreat that reflects the poet's own experience in a literal way, but this does not mean that he presents the withdrawal to the agrarian life of the past as a practical course for others to follow. Indeed, he himself abandoned farming not long after he began to succeed in his literary work. We must remember that he is creating a picture of reality, not drawing up a program, and while the retreat is to be taken literally with reference to the fictional speaker's own life, in terms of the poem it is the symbol of an attitude toward experience, just as New England is the symbol of a way of life.

Frost's apparent lack of concern for the modern world as most readers know it is, then, a consequence of the indirection normal in pastoral, and more broadly, in all poetry. He neither describes the conditions of life in the industrialized urban world, nor has he written much about the specific political and economic problems which are the subject matter of the daily papers. But one may question whether any other major twentieth-century poets, in their best poetry, have done these things either. The poetry most directly concerned with contemporary events, most out-spoken in advocating reform, most engaged in fighting out political battles and plumping for a cause has turned out to be rather second-rate on the whole, as one can see by looking at the poems protesting the horrors of World War I and the radical verse of the Auden circle during the thirties.[9] One finds in Eliot many scenes of drab residential London, Yeats has written of the Irish uprisings, Auden gives us glimpses of both "the peasant river" and "the fash-ionable quays"; yet in each of these poets the modern set-tings are merely parts of a larger picture, whose subject is not the world of 1916, 1922, 1939, or "the modern world" taken as a whole, but a wide historical panorama. It is characteristic of all three to place the modern and the his-torically remote in shocking juxtaposition, thereby per-suading us that Babylon and Bloomsbury are much the same. The result is to deprive the modern materials of their exclusively modern character and to show in the de-bates of the current epoch the elements which have always been present in the human situation. Detachment from controversy and a lack of reforming zeal seem to be com-mon characteristics of modern poets, and they result, not (as some popular reviewers would have us believe) from an inability to deal with modern problems or an indifference to them, but from the feeling that overt argumentation is

9. In speaking of Auden, McNeice, Day Lewis, and Spender, I am here referring only to those of their poems written during the thirties whose primary concern is with contemporary issues. These poems of social conscience, as they may be called, are much less numerous and important than is now generally supposed. This point has been well made recently by John Lehmann in "The Wain-Larkin Myth: A Reply to John Wain," *Sewanee Review*, 66 (1958), 580–1.

not the proper function of poetry. It would be hard to demonstrate that Frost is more aloof from contemporary life than the other major poets.

Lionel Trilling, speaking at a dinner in honor of Frost's eighty-fifth birthday, refuted very effectively this idea of Frost's aloofness. While granting that Frost's "manifest America" seemed distant from the anxieties of our urban society, he found at the center of the poet's work a dominant quality of terror:

> I conceive that Robert Frost is doing in his poems what Lawrence says the great writers of the classic American tradition did. That enterprise of theirs was of an ultimate radicalism. It consisted, Lawrence says, of two things: a disintegration and sloughing off of the old consciousness, by which Lawrence means the old European consciousness, and the forming of a new consciousness underneath.
>
> So radical a work, I need scarcely say, is not carried out by reassurance, nor by the affirmation of old virtues and pieties. It is carried out by the representation of the terrible actualities of life in a new way. I think of Robert Frost as a terrifying poet. . . . The universe that he conceives is a terrifying universe. Read the poem called "Design" and see if you sleep the better for it. Read "Neither Out Far Nor In Deep," which often seems to me the most perfect poem of our time, and see if you are warmed by anything in it except the energy with which emptiness is perceived.[1]

The same grim reality, Trilling goes on to say, is displayed in Frost's characters:

1. I am indebted to Mr. Trilling for supplying me a manuscript copy of his speech, and it is from this that the quotations are taken. The speech has been subsequently published in *Partisan Review, 26* (1959), 445–52.

Talk of the disintegration and sloughing off of the old consciousness! The people of Robert Frost's poems have done that with a vengeance. . . . In the interests of what great other thing these people have made this rejection we cannot know for certain. But we can guess that it was in the interest of truth, of some truth of the self. . . . They affirm *this* of themselves: that they are what they are, that this is their truth, and that if the truth be bare, as truth often is, it is far better than a lie. For me the process by which they arrive at that truth is always terrifying.[2]

One of the great virtues of Trilling's speech is that in it he has made clear the essential way in which Frost's poetry reflects modern life. Frost does not depict the outward events and conditions, but the central facts of twentieth century experience, the uncertainty and painful sense of loss, are there and seem if anything more bleakly apparent in that their social and economic manifestations have been stripped away. More important, Trilling shows us that the terror Frost expresses is the terror which comes and must come with the birth of something new. It is the mark of a genuinely modern poetry.

Subject matter is a poor measure of a poet's modernity. The question is not whether Frost depicts the scenery of modern life, but whether he deals with its major problems. It is a superficial view which would equate these problems with the issues of political campaigns or the questions settled by warfare—the burning issues of one decade are apt to be different from those of the decade before or the decade after. Obviously the poet, if he is going to be truly representative of his age, will have to penetrate the level of social action with its constantly shifting controversy and succession of practical choices to the broad intellectual

2. ibid.

problems which remain unresolved. This I think Frost has done, and done much more bravely, more adventurously, and more perceptively than his readers are yet aware.

Failure to recognize the modernity of Frost's thought is largely due to the fact that his verse lacks the traits of style which seem characteristic of modern poetry. There is what one may call in a very general way a modern style, and although the more one compares poets—Eliot with Yeats or Auden with Cummings, for example—the more differences one sees, nevertheless they do share certain common qualities. Admittedly Frost's manner is different, but it would be absurd to claim that style (in this narrow sense) is the only standard. It is possible to write in the modern idiom and yet show little newness or originality in one's response to the contemporary world. And even among unquestionably fine modern poets one often finds the style a good deal more contemporary than the thought. Stevens' concept of the imagination is apparently derived from Coleridge, and Williams, though he pictures modern conditions very realistically, deals with themes which will not seem entirely new to anyone who has read Walt Whitman attentively. I do not mean that either is at fault. I would merely suggest that if these poets are to be admired for their freshness of manner, then Frost deserves to be admired for his freshness of thought.

The point can best be made by comparing one of Frost's finest recent poems with a sonnet by Dylan Thomas. Thomas' poem is justly admired:

> When all my five and country senses see,
> The fingers will forget green thumbs and mark
> How, through the halfmoon's vegetable eye,
> Husk of young stars and handfull zodiac,
> Love in the frost is pared and wintered by,
> The whispering ears will watch love drummed away

Down breeze and shell to a discordant beach,
And, lashed to syllables, the lynx tongue cry
That her fond wounds are mended bitterly.
My nostrils see her breath burn like a bush.

My one and noble heart has witnesses
In all love's countries, that will grope awake;
And when blind sleep drops on the spying senses,
The heart is sensual, though five eyes break.[3]

That the poem is characteristically modern in form needs no emphasis. The difficulties it presents are of two sorts, and both result from the style. The first arises from the obscurity of syntax. It takes some study to discern the grammatical function of certain words and phrases, for example the antecedent of "her" in "her fond wounds" (line 9). The second, and, I think, more formidable, is that of grasping the many-sided meanings of Thomas' metaphors: "lynx tongue" is easy, but "the halfmoon's vegetable eye,/ Husk of young stars and handfull zodiac" gives one pause. The device of synaesthesia—"The whispering ears will watch" and "My nostrils see"—indicates the kind of compression the poem depends upon, and it is one which leads to a peculiar use of language.

But though the poem has the complexity one expects in modern verse, there is nothing specifically contemporary about what it says. Thomas is here weaving together several familiar and traditional themes. There is, to begin with, the idea that wisdom is the knowledge of death. When the "senses see" what they see is "How . . . Love in the frost is pared and wintered by." The imagery of the octet emphasizes this vision of life diminishing, shrinking back to the primordial seed; hence the tongue will "cry/ That her [love's] fond wounds are mended bitterly"—that

3. *The Collected Poems of Dylan Thomas* (New York, New Directions, 1953), p. 90.

is, through death—and the nostrils "see her breath burn like a bush." The last image suggests not only the perfume of a shrub "ablaze with bloom," but the burning bush of Exodus. The vision is of death—the bush is burnt—but the burning imparts a new insight, just as God revealed his will to Moses. This brings us to the second thematic strand, the idea of life growing out of death. Love does not die out completely; it merely becomes dormant, like the tuber in winter (see again lines 3–5). "And when blind sleep drops on the spying senses,/ The heart is sensual, though five eyes break." One gets the impression that life becomes more intense when it withdraws to its core; as the senses die out in sleep or death, the heart itself becomes "sensual." But the poem does not assert a belief in immortality, or if so, only in a very special sense. Its main theme—to which the other two I have mentioned are subordinate— is that of the unity between the individual (in this case the poet himself) and the natural world. Love binds man to the natural world, because it exists in and through the senses—"country senses," the heart's "witnesses/ In all love's countries." To love is to see through the senses, to see the world of physical decay. In death one loses consciousness by losing the senses, but death is the consummation of love, for then the heart itself is sensual in that the body is merged with the earth. In essence, the poem asserts a monistic view of reality. It portrays man's being, thought, and emotion as organically united to the life-process of the universe, and the resolution which it offers for suffering and death is seen in his reunion with the sum total of things. The central thought is hardly a new one. What is distinctly modern is the way it is presented, most especially Thomas' technique of using images which fuse distant associations, as in "the halfmoon's vegetable eye."

Let us set beside this the two little poems—really one, for they are to be taken together—which Frost has placed at the beginning of *A Witness Tree:*

BEECH

Where my imaginary line
Bends square in woods, an iron spine
And pile of real rocks have been founded.
And off this corner in the wild,
Where these are driven in and piled,
One tree, by being deeply wounded,
Has been impressed as Witness Tree
And made commit to memory
My proof of being not unbounded.
Thus truth's established and borne out,
Though circumstanced with dark and doubt—
Though by a world of doubt surrounded.

THE MOODIE FORESTER

SYCAMORE

Zaccheus he
Did climb the tree
Our Lord to see.

THE NEW ENGLAND PRIMER

The style of this poem lacks the kind of surface complica-
tion we have observed in the sonnet by Thomas. The use
of language is clearer and simpler, the manner more relaxed, and the approach to the reader therefore seems
much more direct. The last three lines of "Beech" can be
taken as a moral or message explaining what the poem
means. As I have argued in previous chapters, Frost's
method is not nearly so simple as it seems, but the effect
is one of simplicity, and by comparing this poem with
Thomas' one sees that its style is less characteristically
modern. With respect to the content, however, the situation is reversed. Whereas Thomas restates traditional
themes in a new way, Frost's theme is distinctively of the
twentieth century.

The poem deals with the nature of conceptualization. Through the image of the "wounded" tree, Frost portrays both the necessity which leads man to form ideas and the loss which the process inevitably involves. The poem is built on the paradox that man, for the purposes of thought, and indeed for life itself, needs abstract symbols which may serve to divide and order reality, yet that these symbols cause suffering and set severe limits to his thought. The beech "by being deeply wounded" establishes the "imaginary line," thus fencing off the human world of the farm from the unordered wilderness beyond. Yet the tree not only, in a sense, creates the farm, it also imprisons man within it—it is the poet's "proof of being not unbounded." This, of course, illustrates the value and limitations of all the imaginary lines or concepts which man creates through symbols. Only by imposing his clear concepts upon the flux of reality can man arrive at certain knowledge, while in turn the hard precision of these concepts restricts his ability to understand.

The fact that Frost calls the beech "Witness Tree" indicates that the poem points beyond man's merely rational thinking to his conceptions of religious truth. Hence the relevance of the lines entitled "Sycamore," which Frost has taken verbatim from *The New England Primer*.[4] The story of Zaccheus serves as a perfect summation of the poem's theme. As presented in the Bible, it illustrates the

---

4. There are slight variations between the numerous editions of the primer. I have not found one in which this verse appears in precisely the form Frost uses, and I do not know whether Frost altered the version he copied. At any rate, such alterations would not be of material importance. In *The New England Primer, Improved: or an Easy and Pleasant Guide to the Art of Reading* (Greenfield, Mass., 1816), the verse appears as follows:

> Zacheus he,
> Did climb the tree,
> His Lord to see.

weakness of man's understanding. Being a short man, Zaccheus climbed a tree in order to get a better view of Christ as he passed—he made the mistake of assuming that to see God meant to see him visibly.[5] Yet this was not entirely a mistake. By his nature man needs a Witness Tree, whether it be the cross, Zaccheus' tree, or the beech which marks the property line.

As I have suggested before, this poem bears the stamp of the present century in a way which the poem by Thomas does not. It bears it more deeply, for it bears it in the thought rather than merely in the form. Frost's view of conceptualization and the role of symbols in human life reflects important strands of thought in modern philosophy, anthropology, and psychology.[6] One feels that the poem could not have been written before the present century. However that may be, the problem with which it deals is relatively new and is still the concern of modern thought, while Thomas in his poem builds upon ideas which at least antedate the Christian era. In saying this, I do not mean to suggest that Frost's poem is better or that Thomas' is any the worse for the ancient pedigree of its thought. Nor is this one illustration meant to establish that Thomas is seldom concerned with specifically modern themes, or that if he were this would be a fault. Modernity does not assure artistic merit. A poem can be typical of the period in which it was written without being good. But those for whom the question of whether or not a poet is representative of his time really matters should notice how consistently and in how original a way Frost has explored major issues of contemporary thought.

The reader will appreciate that the distinction I have made between style and thought in comparing these two

5. Luke 19:2–8.
6. See, for example, Ernst Cassirer, *An Essay on Man* (New York, 1953).

poems is artificial and misleading. It seemed necessary here for the purposes of argument, but, as more than a few have pointed out, the style of a poem and the ideas it expresses are really inseparable. While one must concede that Frost's style does not involve certain obvious, characteristically modern techniques, this does not mean that it is not modern in a fundamental way. Style is the extension into language of a poem's basic structure, and Frost's style, growing as it does from the pastoral design of his verse, displays an indirection and analogical mode of thought which are much more fundamental to modern poetry than any combination of purely verbal devices. The question is not whether his style is modern in precisely the way that Thomas' or Eliot's or Cummings' is, but whether it is modern in its own way—whether it reflects the temper of the age and serves as an idiom for dealing with its most urgent concerns.

While modernity is not in itself a value, there is much to be gained by noting the contemporary nature of Frost's art. The idea of Frost as a poet of the nineteenth century who has somehow got into the twentieth seems absurd when it is brought out into the open, but this phantom image of the poet persists, even in the minds of experienced readers, and it has done much to prevent an intelligent reading of his poems. While the "Beech"–"Sycamore" poem has gone unnoticed, editors of anthologies constantly reprint such poems as "The Runaway," which is not only a much less successful piece, but is not nearly so representative of his thought. Many, in reaction to the popular image of Frost and encouraged by the two essays of Randall Jarrell,[7] have tried to justify their liking for him by pick-

7. Randall Jarrell, "The Other Frost" and "To the Laodicians," *Poetry and The Age* (New York, 1953), pp. 28–36 and 37–69. These originally appeared in *The Nation, 165* (1947), 588–92; and *Kenyon Review, 14* (1952), 535–61, respectively.

ing out for special praise those few poems—mostly lyrics—
which seem "modern" in a superficial sense. Thus currently fashionable ideas about Frost are based upon "Acquainted with the Night," "Design," "Canis Major," "I
Will Sing You One-O," and others of this sort. These are
certainly very fine poems, but they hardly have the scope of
the great regional poems such as "After Apple-Picking" and
"An Old Man's Winter Night," nor are they so representative of his unique achievement. The attempt to remake him
as a metaphysical or Symbolist poet is perverse in the same
way as Eliot's preference of *Coriolanus* to *Hamlet,* and
like the latter, it gives us a valuable insight. It shows how
desperately intelligent readers wish to escape from the
distorted image of Frost foisted on us by popularizers and
sentimental gentlemen who view modern poetry with horror. It is time to exorcize the phantom by recognizing
Frost as the major figure in contemporary literature that
he is.

Whatever Frost's relation to his own age may be, his
achievement, in the end, will be measured by the intrinsic
value of the poems rather than their relevance to the contemporary world. The kind of poetry he writes can best be
understood by observing the method by which he has
sought to make the present moment represent all other
times, and the particular place he describes, the human
situation as it has always existed. His essential technique
is that of pastoral. He has explored wide and manifold
ranges of being by viewing reality within the mirror of
the natural and unchanging world of rural life. Pastoralism, whether in Frost or in the poets of the Arcadian tradition, will always at first appear to involve an escape from
the world as we know it, but actually it is an exploration
upstream, past the city with its riverside factories and
shipping, on against the current of time and change to the
clear waters of the source:

Back out of all this now too much for us,
Back in a time made simple by the loss
Of detail, burned, dissolved, and broken off
Like graveyard marble sculpture in the weather,
There is a house that is no more a house
Upon a farm that is no more a farm
And in a town that is no more a town.
The road there, if you'll let a guide direct you
Who only has at heart your getting lost,
May seem as if it should have been a quarry— . . .

Your destination and your destiny's
A brook that was the water of the house,
Cold as a spring as yet so near its source,
Too lofty and original to rage.
(We know the valley streams that when aroused
Will leave their tatters hung on barb and thorn.)
I have kept hidden in the instep arch
Of an old cedar at the waterside
A broken drinking goblet like the Grail
Under a spell so the wrong ones can't find it,
So can't get saved, as Saint Mark says they mustn't.
(I stole the goblet from the children's playhouse.)
Here are your waters and your watering place.
Drink and be whole again beyond confusion.[8]

8. "Directive."

BIBLIOGRAPHY

PART I: A SELECT BIBLIOGRAPHY
OF WORKS BY FROST

1. The Major Volumes

A Boy's Will: London, Nutt, 1913; New York, Holt, 1915.
North of Boston: London, Nutt, 1914; New York, Holt, 1915.
Mountain Interval, New York, Holt, 1916.
New Hampshire: A Poem with Notes and Grace Notes, New York, Holt, 1923.
West-Running Brook, New York, Holt, 1928.
A Further Range, New York, Holt, 1936.
A Witness Tree, New York, Holt, 1942.
A Masque of Reason, New York, Holt, 1945.
A Masque of Mercy, New York, Holt, 1947.
Steeple Bush, New York, Holt, 1947.

2. Some Important Collected Editions

Selected Poems, New York, Holt, 1923.
Selected Poems, rev. ed., New York, Holt, 1928.
Collected Poems of Robert Frost, New York, Holt, 1930.
Selected Poems, 3rd ed., New York, Holt, 1934.
Selected Poems, ed. Robert Frost, London, Jonathan Cape, 1936.
Introductory essays by W. H. Auden, C. Day Lewis, Paul Engle, and Edwin Muir.
Collected Poems of Robert Frost: 1939, New York, Holt, 1939.
Come In and Other Poems, ed. Louis Untermeyer, New York, Holt, 1943.
The Pocket Book of Robert Frost's Poems, ed. Louis Untermeyer, New York, Pocket Books, 1946.
The Poems of Robert Frost, New York, Modern Library Edition, 1946.
Complete Poems of Robert Frost: 1949, New York, Holt, 1949.

Complete Poems, New York, Limited Editions Club, 1950.
The Road Not Taken: An Introduction to Robert Frost, ed. Louis
Untermeyer, New York, Holt, 1951.
Aforesaid, ed. Robert Frost, New York, Holt, 1954. Limited edition.

3. Miscellaneous Poetry

"A Dream of Julius Caesar," Lawrence, Mass. *High School Bulletin*
(April 1890), p. 1.
"La Noche Triste '92," Lawrence, Mass. *High School Bulletin* (May
1890), p. 3.
"Song of the Wave," Lawrence, Mass. *High School Bulletin* (May
1890), p. 3.
"Class Hymn," Lawrence, Mass. *High School Bulletin* (June 1892),
p. 10.
"The Birches Do Thus," *Independent, 48* (August 20, 1896), 1.
"Caesar's Lost Transport Ships," *Independent, 49* (January 14,
1897), 1.
"Warning," *Independent, 49* (September 9, 1897), 1.
"The Lost Faith," Derry, N. H. *Derry News,* March 1, 1907.
"Across the Atlantic," *Independent, 64* (March 26, 1908), 676.
"The Return of the Pilgrims," in George P. Barker, *The Pilgrim
Spirit,* Boston, Marshall Jones, 1921.
"The Middletown Murder," *Saturday Review of Literature, 5* (Oc-
tober 13, 1928), 216.
The Cow's in the Corn, Gaylordsville, Slide Mountain Press, 1929.
A one-act play.
"Winter Ownership," *New York Herald Tribune Magazine* (March 4,
1934), p. 12.
"Good Relief," in *Come Christmas: A Selection of Christmas Poetry,*
ed. Lesley Frost (New York, Coward-McCann, 1935), pp. 4–5.
"Once Down on My Knees," in *Fifty Years of Robert Frost: A
Catalogue of the Exhibition held in Baker Library in the Autumn
of 1943,* ed. Ray Nash, Hanover, N. H., Dartmouth College Library,
1944.
"But He Meant It," *Atlantic Monthly, 179* (April 1947), 55.
"Doom to Bloom," New York, Holt, 1950.
Hard Not to Be King, New York, House of Books, 1951.
"And All We Call American," *Atlantic Monthly, 187* (June 1951),
28–9.
"Cabin in the Clearing," New York, Spiral Press, 1951. A Christmas
card.

"Does No One but Me at All Ever Feel This Way in the Least . . . ," New York, Spiral Press, 1952. A Christmas card.

"One More Brevity," New York, Spiral Press, 1953. A Christmas card.

"From a Milkweed Pod," New York, Spiral Press, 1954. A Christmas card.

"Some Science Fiction," New York, Spiral Press, 1954. A Christmas card.

"Kitty Hawk," *Atlantic Monthly, 200* (November 1957), 52–6.

"My Objection to Being Stepped On," New York, Spiral Press, 1955. A Christmas card.

"Of a Winter Evening," *Saturday Review of Literature, 41* (April 12, 1958), 66.

"Away!" New York, Spiral Press, 1958. A Christmas card.

"A-Wishing Well," New York, Spiral Press, 1959. A Christmas card.

"Somewhat Dietary," *Massachusetts Review, 1* (October 1959), 24.

4. Miscellaneous Prose

Preface to *Memoirs of the Notorious Stephen Burroughs of New Hampshire* (New York, Dial Press, 1924), pp. v–viii.

"Vocal Imagination," *Lewiston (Maine) Evening Journal* (May 5, 1925), p. 3.

"The Poetry of Amy Lowell," *Christian Science Monitor* (May 6, 1925), p. 8.

Introduction to *The Arts Anthology: Dartmouth Verse, 1925* (Portland, Maine, Mosher, 1925), pp. vii–ix.

A Way Out, New York, Harbor Press, 1929. A one-act play.

"Education by Poetry: A Meditative Monologue," *Amherst Graduates' Quarterly, 20* (February 1931), 75–85. A lecture.

Introduction to Edwin Arlington Robinson, *King Jasper* (New York, Macmillan, 1935), pp. v–xv.

"Poverty and Poetry," *Biblia* (published by Friends of Princeton Library), *9* (February 1938), n.p. A lecture.

"The Poet's Next of Kin in a College," *Biblia* (published by Friends of Princeton Library), *9* (February 1938), n.p.

The Guardeen. Los Angeles, Ward Ritchie Press, 1943. The first act of a play. Prose?

"Speaking of Loyalty," *Amherst Graduates' Quarterly, 37* (August 1948), 271–76. A lecture.

"Poetry and School," *Atlantic Monthly, 187* (June 1951), 30–1.

"A Poet, Too, Must Learn the Magic Way of Poetry": *New York Times Book Review* (March 21, 1954), p. 1; preface to the limited

edition of Frost, *Aforesaid,* ed. Robert Frost, New York, Holt, 1954.
Introduction to Sidney Cox, *A Swinger of Birches: A Portrait of Robert Frost* (New York, New York Univ. Press, 1957), pp. vii–viii.
Introduction to *New Poets of England and America,* ed. Donald Hall et al. (New York, Meridian Books, 1957), pp. 10–12.
With C. Day Lewis: "It Takes a Hero to Make a Poem," *Claremont Quarterly,* 5 (Spring 1958), 27–34. Conversation broadcast over the BBC.

PART II: A SELECT BIBLIOGRAPHY
OF WORKS ABOUT FROST
AND HIS POETRY

1. Books

Cook, Reginald L., *The Dimensions of Robert Frost,* New York, Rinehart, 1959. Contains records of conversation.
Cox, Sidney, *A Swinger of Birches: A Portrait of Robert Frost,* with an introduction by Robert Frost, New York, New York Univ. Press, 1957. Contains records of conversation.
—— *Robert Frost: Original "Ordinary Man,"* New York, Holt, 1929.
Ford, Caroline, *The Less Travelled Road,* Cambridge, Mass., Harvard Univ. Press, 1935. Harvard master's thesis.
Munson, Gorham B., *Robert Frost: A Study in Sensibility and Good Sense,* New York, George H. Doran, 1927.
Recognition of Robert Frost: Twenty-fifth Anniversary, ed. Richard Thornton, New York, Holt, 1937. Important collection of early criticism.
Thompson, Lawrance, *Fire and Ice: The Art and Thought of Robert Frost,* New York, Holt, 1942.

2. Essays and Articles

A. GENERAL VIEWS

Aykroyd, George O., "The Classical in Robert Frost," *Poet-Lore, 40* (Winter 1929), 610–14.
Baker, Carlos, "Frost on the Pumpkin," *Georgia Review, 11* (Summer 1957), 117–31.
Beach, Joseph Warren, "Robert Frost," *Yale Review, 43* (Winter 1954), 204–17.

Berkelman, Robert G., "Robert Frost and the Middle Way," *College English, 3* (January 1942), 347–53.

Bracker, Milton, "The 'Quietly Overwhelming' Robert Frost," *New York Times Magazine Section* (November 30, 1958), pp. 15, 57, 59, 62.

Brooks, Cleanth, "Frost, MacLeish, and Auden," in *Modern Poetry and the Tradition* (Chapel Hill, Univ. of North Carolina Press, 1939), pp. 110–35.

Coffin, Robert P. Tristram, *New Poetry of New England: Frost and Robinson*, Baltimore, Johns Hopkins Press, 1938.

Cook, Reginald L., "Frost on Frost: The Making of Poems," *American Literature, 28* (March 1956), 62–72.

Cowley, Malcolm, "Frost: A Dissenting Opinion," *New Republic, 111* (Sept. 11 and 18, 1944), 312–13, 345–7.

Cox, James M., "Robert Frost and the Edge of the Clearing," *Virginia Quarterly Review, 35* (Winter 1959), 73–88.

Cox, Sidney, "Robert Frost and Poetic Fashion," *American Scholar, 18* (Winter 1948–49), 78–86.

De Voto, Bernard, "The Critics and Robert Frost," *Saturday Review of Literature, 17* (Jan. 1, 1938), 3–4, 14–15.

Fletcher, John Gould, "Robert Frost the Outlander," *Mark Twain Quarterly, 3* (Spring 1940), 5–8.

Foster, Charles Howell, "Robert Frost and the New England Tradition," *Elizabethan Studies and Other Essays in Honor of George F. Reynolds, University of Colorado Studies*, ser. B, 2 (Boulder, Colorado, October 1945), 370–81. Reply to Malcolm Cowley; *see entry above.*

Greene, Marc T., "Robert Frost at Home," *Poetry Review* (London), *47* (January–March 1956), 16–18.

Heywood, Terence, "Homage to Frost," *Poetry Review, 31* (March–April 1940), 129–35.

Jarrell, Randall, "The Other Robert Frost" and "To the Laodiceans," in *Poetry and the Age* (New York, Knopf, 1953), pp. 28–36, 37–69.

Kreymbourg, Alfred, "The Fire and Ice of Robert Frost," in *Our Singing Strength* (New York, Coward-McCann, 1929), pp. 316–22.

Long, William S., "Frost," *C.E.A. Critic, 10* (November 1948), 4.

Lord, Richard D., "Frost and Cyclicism," *Renascence, 10* (Autumn 1957), 19–25, 31.

Lowell, Amy, "Robert Frost," in *Tendencies in Modern American Poetry* (New York, Macmillan, 1917), pp. 79–136.

Monroe, Harriet, "Robert Frost," in *Poets and Their Art* (New York, Macmillan, 1926), pp. 56–62.

Montgomery, Marion, "Robert Frost and His Use of Barriers: Man vs. Nature toward God," *South Atlantic Quarterly, 57* (Summer 1958), 339–53.

Mulder, William, "Freedom and Form: Robert Frost's Double Discipline," *South Atlantic Quarterly, 54* (July 1955), 386–93.

Munson, Gorham B., "Robert Frost and the Humanistic Temper," *Bookman, 71* (July 1930), 419–22.

Napier, John T., "A Momentary Stay against Confusion," *Virginia Quarterly Review, 33* (Summer 1957), 378–94.

New Hampshire Troubadour, 16 (November 1946). A "Frost Issue," it contains several brief articles on the poet.

O'Donnell, William G., "Robert Frost and New England: A Revaluation," *Yale Review, 37* (Summer 1948), 698–712.

Ogilvie, John T., "From Woods to Stars: A Pattern of Imagery in Robert Frost's Poetry," *South Atlantic Quarterly, 58* (Winter 1959), 64–76.

Papajewski, Helmut, "Grundzüge und Substrat in der Lyrik Robert Frosts," *Archiv für das Studium des neueren Sprachen und Literaturen, 193* (October 1956), 113–28.

Pearce, Roy Harvey, "The Poet as Person," *Yale Review, 41* (Spring 1952), 419–40.

Russell, Francis, "Frost in the Evening," *Horizon, 1* (November 1958), 34–5.

Sergeant, Howard, "The Poetry of Robert Frost," *English, 9* (Spring 1952), 13–16.

Thompson, Lawrance, "A Native to the Grain of the American Idiom," *Saturday Review of Literature, 42* (March 21, 1959), 21, 55–6.

Thorpe, Willard, "The 'New Poetry,'" *Literary History of the United States,* ed. Robert E. Spiller et al. 2 vols. (New York, Macmillan, 1949), 2, 1189–96.

Trilling, Lionel, "A Speech on Robert Frost: A Cultural Episode," *Partisan Review, 26* (Summer 1959), 445–52.

Untermeyer, Louis, "The Northwest Corner," in *From Another World: The Autobiography of Louis Untermeyer* (New York, Harcourt, 1939), pp. 206–28.

———— "Robert Frost," in *American Poetry since 1900* (New York, Holt, 1923), pp. 15–41.

———— "Robert Frost," in *The New Era in American Poetry* (New York, Holt, 1919), pp. 15–39.

Van Doren, Carl, "The Soil of the Puritans," in *Many Minds* (New York, Knopf, 1924), pp. 50–66.

Van Doren, Mark, "Robert Frost's America," *Atlantic Monthly, 187* (June 1951), 32–4.

Viereck, Peter, "Parnassus Divided," *Atlantic Monthly, 184* (October 1949), 67–8.

Waggoner, Hyatt Howe, "The Humanistic Idealism of Robert Frost," *American Literature, 13* (November 1941), 207–33.

Watts, Harold H., "Robert Frost and the Interrupted Dialogue," *American Literature, 27* (March 1955), 69–87.

——— "Three Entities and Robert Frost," *Bucknell Review, 5* (December 1955), 19–38.

Wellek, René and Austin Warren: brief discussion of Frost's symbolism in "Image, Metaphor, Symbol, Myth," in *Theory of Literature* (New York, Harcourt, 1949), pp. 194–95.

Wells, Henry W., "Nearer and Farther Ranges," in *The American Way of Poetry* (New York, Columbia Univ. Press, 1943), pp. 106–21.

Winters, Yvor, "Robert Frost: Or the Spiritual Drifter as Poet," *Sewanee Review, 56* (Autumn 1948), 564–96.

Wood, Clement, "Robert Frost: The Twilight of New England," in *Poets of America* (New York, Dutton, 1925), pp. 142–62.

B. EXPLICATIONS ARRANGED ALPHABETICALLY BY POEM

"Acquainted with the Night": Malcolm Brown, "The Sweet Crystalline Cry," *Western Review, 16* (Summer 1952), 259–74.

"After Apple-Picking": Cleanth Brooks and Robert Penn Warren, in *Understanding Poetry,* rev. ed. (New York, Holt, 1951), pp. 389–97.

"Beech" (and "Sycamore"): Alvan S. Ryan, *Explicator, 7* (March 1949), item 39.

"Brown's Descent": Walter Gierasch, *Explicator, 11* (June 1953), item 60.

"Come In": Robert Ornstein, *Explicator, 15* (June 1957), item 61.

"The Death of the Hired Man": Bess Cooper Hopkins, "A Study of 'The Death of the Hired Man,'" *English Journal, 43* (April 1954), 175–6, 186; Charles C. Walcutt, *Explicator, 3* (October 1944), item 7.

"Desert Places": Cleanth Brooks and Robert Penn Warren, in *Understanding Poetry,* rev. ed. (New York, Holt, 1951), pp. 87–8.

"Devotion": Walter Gierasch, *Explicator, 10* (May 1952), item 50.

198   THE PASTORAL ART OF ROBERT FROST

"Directive": Mildred E. Harstock, *Explicator, 16* (April 1958), item 42.

"Dust of Snow": Hans Combecher, "Versuch einer Interpretation von vier Gedichten des Neuengländers Robert Lee Frost," *Die neueren Sprachen, 6* (June 1957), 281–89.

"Fire and Ice": *see entry above under* "Dust of Snow."

"The Last Mowing": Walter Gierasch, *Explicator, 10* (February 1952), item 25.

"The Lone Striker": Frederick L. Gwynn, "Poetry Crisis at Corning," *C.E.A. Critic, 15* (December 1953), 1, 3. A panel discussion.

"The Lovely Shall Be Choosers": E. Nitchie and M. L. Werner, *Explicator, 13* (May 1955), item 39; Edward Schwartz, *Explicator, 13* (October 1954), item 3.

"A Masque of Mercy": Sister Mary Jeremy Finnegan, "Frost's 'Masque of Mercy,' " *Catholic World, 186* (February 1958), 357–61; William G. O'Donnell, "Parable in Poetry," *Virginia Quarterly Review, 25* (Spring 1949), 269–82.

"A Masque of Reason": Hyatt Howe Waggoner, *Explicator, 4* (March 1948), item 32.

"Mending Wall": John C. Broderick, *Explicator, 14* (January 1956), item 24.

"Mowing": *see entry above under* "Dust of Snow."

"The Need of Being Versed in Country Things": Cleanth Brooks et al., in *An Approach to Literature,* 3rd ed. (New York, Appleton, 1952), pp. 346–7.

"Neither Out Far nor In Deep": Lawrence Perrine, *Explicator, 7* (April 1949), item 46; R. W. Stallman, "The Position of Poetry Today," *English Journal, 46* (May 1957), 241–51.

"Once by the Pacific": Reuben A. Brower, *The Fields of Light: An Experiment in Critical Reading* (New York, Oxford Univ. Press, 1951), pp. 21–23.

"The Road Not Taken": Ben W. Griffith, Jr., *Explicator, 12* (June 1954), item 55.

"Sand Dunes": Lawrence Perrine, *Explicator, 14* (March 1956), item 38.

"Sitting by a Bush in Broad Sunlight": H. M. Campbell, *Explicator, 5* (December 1946), item 18.

"Stopping by Woods on a Snowy Evening": John Ciardi, "Robert Frost: The Way to The Poem," *Saturday Review of Literature, 41* (April 12, 1958), 13–15, 65; Hans Combecher, *see entry above under* "Dust of Snow"; Charles A. McLaughlin, "Two Views of Poetic Unity," *University of Kansas City Review, 22* (June 1956),

309–16; Leonard Unger and William Van O'Connor, *Poems for Study: A Critical and Historical Introduction* (New York, Rinehart, 1953), pp. 597–600; Charles C. Walcutt, "Interpreting the Symbol," *College English, 14* (May 1953), 446–54.

"The Subverted Flower": Howard Mumford, *Explicator, 17* (January 1959), item 31; Donald B. Stauffer, *Explicator, 15* (March 1957), item 38.

"To Earthward": Wilbur S. Scott, *Explicator, 16* (January 1958), item 23.

"Two Tramps in Mud Time": Charles Kaplan, *Explicator, 12* (June 1954), item 51.

"West-Running Brook": H. T. Webster, *Explicator, 8* (February 1950), item 32.

"The Wood-Pile": Cleanth Brooks et al., in *An Approach to Literature*, 3rd ed. (New York, Appleton, 1952), pp. 305–7.

C. SPECIAL SUBJECTS

Archibald, R. O., "The Year of Frost's Birth," *Notes and Queries, 199* (January 1954), 40.

Barre, Michel, "Robert Frost en France," *Le Bayou* (Houston), *23* (Spring 1959), 289–97.

Chatman, Seymour, "Robert Frost's 'Mowing': An Inquiry into Prosodic Structure," *Kenyon Review, 18* (Summer 1956), 421–38.

Ciardi, John, "Robert Frost, Master Conversationalist," *Saturday Review of Literature, 42* (March 21, 1959), 17–20, 54.

Cook, Reginald L., "Emerson and Frost: A Parallel of Seers," *New England Quarterly, 31* (June 1958), 200–17.

———— "Frost as Parabalist," *Accent, 10* (Autumn 1949), 33–41.

———— "Frost Country," *Vermont Life, 3* (Summer 1949), 15–17.

———— "Frost on Analytical Criticism," *College English, 17* (May 1956), 434–8.

———— "Notes on Frost the Lecturer," *Quarterly Journal of Speech, 42* (April 1956), 127–32.

———— "Robert Frost: A Time to Listen," *College English, 7* (November 1945), 66–71.

———— "Robert Frost's Asides on His Poetry," *American Literature, 19* (January 1948), 351–9.

Cox, Sidney, "New England and Robert Frost," *New Mexico Quarterly, 4* (May 1934), 89–94.

Eckert, Robert P., Jr., "Robert Frost in England," *Mark Twain Quarterly, 3* (Spring 1940), 14–16.

Farjon, Eleanor, "Edward Thomas and Robert Frost," *London Magazine, 1* (May 1954), 50–61.

Landré, Louis, "Premières Critiques de Robert Frost," *Etudes Anglaises, 5* (May 1952), 136–46.

Moynihan, William T., "Fall and Winter in Frost," *Modern Language Notes, 83* (May 1958), 348–50.

Newdick, Robert S., "The Early Verse of Robert Frost and Some of His Revisions," *American Literature, 7* (May 1935), 181–7.

———— "Robert Frost and the Sound of Sense," *American Literature, 9* (November 1937), 289–300.

———— "Robert Frost's Other Harmony," *Sewanee Review, 48* (July–September 1940), 409–18.

Ryan, Alvan S., "Frost and Emerson: Voice and Vision," *Massachusetts Review, 1* (October 1959), 5–23.

Yates, Norris, "An Instance of Parallel Imagery in Hawthorne, Melville, and Frost," *Philological Quarterly, 36* (April 1957), 276–80.

D. REVIEWS

Anonymous, review of *North of Boston, Independent, 82* (May 31, 1915), 638.

———— review of *Selected Poems,* New York, Holt, 1923 in (London) *Times Literary Supplement* (March 29, 1923), p. 213.

———— "The Poetry of Robert Frost," (London) *Times Literary Supplement* (March 9, 1951), p. 148.

Blackmur, R. P., "The Instincts of a Bard," *Nation, 142* (June 24, 1936), 817–19. Review of *A Further Range.*

Daiches, David, review of *Complete Poems: 1949,* New York, Holt, 1949, in *New York Times Book Review, 54* (May 29, 1949), 1, 13.

Dudley, Dorothy, "The Acid Text," *Poetry, 23* (March 1924), 328–35. Review of *New Hampshire.*

Dupee, F. W., review of *A Masque of Reason* in *Nation, 160* (April 21, 1945), 464–5.

Firkins, O. W., review of *A Boy's Will* in *Nation, 101* (August 19, 1915), 228.

Forgotson, E. S., review of *A Masque of Reason* in *Poetry, 66* (June 1945), 156–9.

Henderson, Alice C., review of *North of Boston* in *Dial, 57* (October 1914), 254.

Hicks, Granville, review of *Collected Poems,* New York, Holt, 1930, in *New Republic, 65* (December 3, 1930), 77–8.

Hillyer, Robert, review of *A Witness Tree* in *Atlantic Monthly, 169*

(June 1942), n.p. In a survey of books entitled "Atlantic Bookshelf," an unfolioed section in the forepages.

—— review of *A Masque of Mercy* in *Saturday Review of Literature, 30* (December 6, 1947), 54–6.

McMillen, L., "A Modern Allegory," *Hudson Review, 1* (Spring 1948), 105–7. Review of *A Masque of Reason*.

Morton, David, "The Poet of the New Hampshire Hills," *Outlook, 135* (December 19, 1923), 688–89. Review of *New Hampshire*.

Payne, W. M., review of *A Boy's Will* in *Dial, 55* (September 16, 1913), 21.

Rittenhouse, Jesse B., review of *North of Boston* in *New York Times Review of Books* (May 16, 1915), p. 189.

Rukeyser, Muriel, review of *Collected Poems: 1939*, New York, Holt, 1939, in *Poetry, 54* (July 1939), 218–24.

Schneider, Isidor, review of *Collected Poems*, New York, Holt, 1930, in *Nation, 132* (January 28, 1931), 101–2.

Shorer, Mark, review of *A Masque of Reason* in *Atlantic Monthly, 175* (March 1945), 133.

Spencer, Theodore, "West-Running Brook," *New Republic, 58* (February 20, 1929), 24–25.

Wheelwright, John, review of *A Further Range*, in *Poetry, 49* (October 1936), 45–8.

E. BIBLIOGRAPHIES

Anonymous, *An Exhibition of the Work of Robert Frost*, Meadville, Pennsylvania, Allegheny College, 1938.

Arms, George and Joseph M. Kuntz, list of explications of Frost poems in *Poetry Explication* (New York, Swallow Press and Morrow, 1950), pp. 76–8.

Clymer, W. B. Shubrick and Charles R. Green, *Robert Frost: A Bibliography*, Amherst, Mass., Jones Library, 1937. A descriptive bibliography of publications by Frost.

Mertins, Louis and Esther, *The Intervals of Robert Frost: A Critical Bibliography*, Berkeley, Univ. of California Press, 1947. Contains a detailed description of items in the Mertins' collection, collations, information on first publication, biographical and critical commentary. Invaluable, though somewhat confused.

Nash, Ray, ed., *Fifty Years of Robert Frost: A Catalogue of the Exhibition held in Baker Library in the Autumn of 1943*, Hanover, N. H., Dartmouth College Library, 1944.

Newdick, Robert S., "Foreign Response to Robert Frost," *Colophon, 2* (Winter 1937), 289–90.

Thompson, Lawrance, *Robert Frost: A Chronological Survey: Compiled in connection with an exhibit of his work at the Olin Memorial Library, Wesleyan University, April, 1936,* Middletown, Conn., Olin Memorial Library, 1936.

West, Herbert Faulkneer, "My Robert Frost Collection," in *The Mind on The Wing: A Book for Readers and Collectors,* New York, Coward-McCann, 1947.

INDEX

YALE STUDIES IN ENGLISH

This volume is the one hundred and forty-seventh of the Yale Studies in English, founded by Albert Stanburrough Cook in 1898 and edited by him until his death in 1927. Tucker Brooke succeeded him as editor, and served until 1941, when Benjamin C. Nangle succeeded him.

The following volumes are still in print. Orders should be addressed to YALE UNIVERSITY PRESS, New Haven, Connecticut.